Praise for *Born to Wander*

We are all wanderers, whether literal, figurative—or both. With wisdom as deep as the waters of the sea and prose as sharp as the needle of a compass, Michelle Van Loon guides her readers out of exile and back into the arms of God—our only true home.

KAREN SWALLOW PRIOR
Author of *On Reading Well* and *Fierce Convictions: The Extraordinary Life of Hannah More—Poet, Reformer, Abolitionist*

There's nothing quite like knowing where you belong in the world, but in an age of constant change, sudden shifts, and unexpected transitions, this is an increasingly elusive experience. In *Born to Wander*, Michelle Van Loon writes to all those who can't quite seem to find their place, offering hope that our restlessness echoes a more significant journey. Drawing on Scripture and her own history, Van Loon reminds us that as much as we're making our way through this life, we're also making our way to Him—and in finding Him, we'll finally find our way home.

HANNAH ANDERSON
Author of *Humble Roots: How Humility Grounds and Nourishes Your Soul*

Born to Wander is a book about pilgrimage, and a pilgrimage itself. A readable, engaging journey through the Old Testament, interwoven with truths about Jesus and insights about pilgrimage, *Born to Wander* took me on new paths, provided new insights, engaged my heart, mind, and soul. Readers will learn more about the Bible, but also and what it means to follow Jesus—that is, to pilgrimage. Themes of remembering, exile, worship, lament, repentance, obedience are interwoven with candid self-revelations and unexpected connections. Readers will see their own story in this pilgrimage through God's story. Michelle Van Loon's unique perspective as a Jewish follower of Jesus makes her the perfect guide for this journey, and she's obviously intimately familiar with these paths through the Scriptures. Study questions for each chapter makes this a great resource for groups or individual deeper study.

KERI WYATT KENT
Author of *GodSpace: Embracing the Inconvenient Adventure of Intimacy with God*

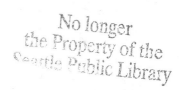

Born to Wander is a beautiful book. In its pages, Michelle Van Loon connects the universal instinct to wander to the Bible's theme of pilgrimage. Van Loon understands that wandering is a double-edged sword, prompted both by a thirst for adventure and an unfulfilled longing for home, "the ache of the uprooted plant." Her lyrical, wide-ranging exploration of the topic will help you find meaning in your own journey, no matter how halting and haphazard it has seemed to be. As she observes, "You were born—and born again—to wander."

DREW DYCK
Contributing editor at CTPastors.com, and author of *Your Future Self Will Thank You: Secrets to Self-Control from the Bible and Brain Science*

Michelle's poignant storytelling draws in readers with insight for the unrest and discontent we often feel in our lives. She reminds us of the pilgrim nature of the lives of every generation of believers and leaves those who have experienced the kinds of struggles that uproot and displace us with a practical theology for understanding it. We may be wanderers, but we are wandering toward home, drawn by our good Father who hasn't left us as orphans to wander alone.

WENDY ALSUP
Author of *Is the Bible Good for Women?: Seeking Clarity and Confidence Through a Jesus-centered Understanding of Scripture*

Born to Wander is a rich and generous call to the ancient but increasingly resonant pilgrim way. Threading together Israel's exile and sojourn in the wilderness with Jesus' troubling call to walk in the way of the cross, Michelle Van Loon beautifully illumines the wandering character of the Christian life. In a time when many Christians hope and expect that Jesus lived, died, and rose again to make them immediately and temporally happy, Van Loon's experience as a Jewish Christian, and her own wayfaring in the sometime spiritual desert of evangelicalism, provides a warm and gracious invitation to follow Jesus on His own terms, to a better country.

ANNE CARLSON KENNEDY
Author of *Nailed It: 365 Sarcastic Devotions for Angry or Worn-Out People*

As a "retail gypsy," I moved roughly every two years as my father climbed the management ladder of a major retail company. So it's fair to say I'm well acquainted with rootlessness. Even now, I feel the urge to move, to see what God has in store down the road. That, according to Michelle Van Loon, is a holy urge, a God-inspired impulse to transform from mere wanderer to true pilgrim and to find the place where traveling will cease. That message is the beating heart of *Born to Wander*, and in its pages, readers will find a map for the journey. She has created a Scripture-rich guidebook to help us all as we go.

JAMIE A. HUGHES
Writer and editor

A friend of mine recently encouraged me with these words: "It's easy to follow God's will if we're willing to go anywhere." That's the pilgrim concept found throughout the Bible and it's an essential requirement for serving our King-Messiah. Michelle Van Loon, with biblical insight, encouraging stories, and an engaging style, leads us into grappling with what it means to follow the King wherever He leads. *Born to Wander* will encourage our hearts while drawing us closer to Messiah Jesus. Don't miss it.

MICHAEL RYDELNIK
Professor of Jewish Studies and Bible, Moody Bible Institute
Host and Teacher, Open Line with Dr. Michael Rydelnik, Moody Radio

The rootlessness and restlessness that accompany so many of us through life can feel, at best, like a burden. Michelle Van Loon begs to differ. Her beautiful new book reorients us toward finding our pilgrim status not a burden, but a blessing from God.

GINA DALFONZO
Author of *One by One: Welcoming the Singles in Your Church*

The world is made up of pioneers and settlers. God never called us to settle. In the words of Michelle Van Loon, we were born to wander. This book will show you how to wander well.

DAN STANFORD
Pastor and author of *Losing the Cape: The Power of Ordinary in a World of Superheroes*

I've moved eighteen times in eighteen years and never have I ever felt so understood as I have reading *Born to Wander*. For the wanderer by chance or choice, circumstances beyond your control or thought to be within your control, this book is for you. Taking her readers on a journey through Scripture, Michelle Van Loon topples the Western idol of home and points instead to the home written on the hearts of all: eternity with God. If you have felt prone to wander or simply born to wander, I hope this book will encourage you as it has me.

LORE FERGUSON WILBERT
Writer at Sayable.net and assorted other publications

We are all exiles trying to find our way back to Eden. Van Loon sagely teaches us that the remedy for our longing will not come by pursuing security or comfort, but rather by living as pilgrims, who faithfully follow the Father's call.

DOROTHY LITTELL GRECO
Photographer, writer, and author of *Making Marriage Beautiful*

Born *to* WANDER

RECOVERING THE VALUE OF OUR PILGRIM IDENTITY

Michelle Van Loon

MOODY PUBLISHERS

CHICAGO

All Scripture quotations, unless otherwise indicated, are taken from the Holy Bible, New International Version®, NIV®. Copyright © 1973, 1978, 1984, 2011 by Biblica, Inc.™ Used by permission of Zondervan. All rights reserved worldwide. www.zondervan.com. The "NIV" and "New International Version" are trademarks registered in the United States Patent and Trademark Office by Biblica, Inc.™

Scripture quotations marked KJV are taken from the King James Version.

Names and details of some stories have been changed to protect the privacy of individuals.

Edited by Amanda Cleary Eastep
Interior design: Erik M. Peterson
Cover design: Connie Gabbert Design and Illustration
Author photo: Gini Lange Images

Published in association with the literary agency The Steve Laube Agency, 24 W. Camelback Rd. A635, Phoenix, AZ 85013.

Library of Congress Cataloging-in-Publication Data

Names: Van Loon, Michelle, author.
Title: Born to wander : recovering the value of our pilgrim identity /
  Michelle Van Loon.
Description: Chicago : Moody Publishers, 2018. | Includes bibliographical
  references.
Identifiers: LCCN 2018009911 (print) | LCCN 2018022399 (ebook) | ISBN
  9780802496447 (ebook) | ISBN 9780802418128
Subjects: LCSH: Identity (Psychology)--Religious aspects--Christianity. |
  Strangers--Religious aspects--Christianity. | Change
  (Psychology)--Religious aspects--Christianity.
Classification: LCC BV4509.5 (ebook) | LCC BV4509.5 .V356 2018 (print) | DDC
  248.4--dc23
LC record available at https://lccn.loc.gov/2018009911

ISBN-13: 978-0-8024-1812-8

We hope you enjoy this book from Moody Publishers. Our goal is to provide high-quality, thought-provoking books and products that connect truth to your real needs and challenges. For more information on other books and products written and produced from a biblical perspective, go to www.moodypublishers.com or write to:

Moody Publishers
820 N. LaSalle Boulevard
Chicago, IL 60610

1 3 5 7 9 10 8 6 4 2

Printed in the United States of America

"Blessed are those whose strength is in you,
whose hearts are set on pilgrimage."

PSALM 84:5

CONTENTS

INTRODUCTION

I've lived a tumbleweed life. I've had sixteen addresses. I've been employed at ten full-time jobs, eight part-time jobs, and a bushel basketful of freelance gigs. I've belonged to twenty churches and visited too many to count as I've searched for a congregational home I know will be home only until it's time to relocate once again.

I was born to wander.

You might say wandering is in my blood. My forebears learned many generations ago that being anchored in a community was a luxury reserved for others. We learned to ply a life from the rickety throwaway homes that existed at the ragged edges of other cultures, always aware that at any moment, it might be time to leave or else be killed. Without realizing why, I learned early on to keep a stash of battered moving boxes on hand. You never know when it might be time to use them.

I've known people who are as rooted to their land as a hundred-year oak. They've lived in the same place for generations, in vintage homes and communities as predictable as a grandfather clock. Though Americans are a people on the move (11 percent of Americans will relocate this year[1]), 40 percent of us will live our entire lives in our hometown.[2] If they're honest, most will affirm there is a sense of restlessness residing in their souls that has nothing to do with how long they've lived at their current address.

I've known others who will never have the privilege of naming that restlessness from the relative comfort of a specific place. They've been uprooted from homes and communities because of famine or war—or both. Some estimate there are as many as sixty million people on planet Earth who've been forcibly displaced.[3] It's safe to say the lion's share would not have chosen this plotline for their story.

Every one of us carries a restlessness that runs as deep as the marrow of our born-again bones. Our relationships shift like tectonic plates. We change jobs. We switch churches. And our culture tells us the cure for our restlessness is to buy a new mattress, a new car, or a new tube of toothpaste.

But we know that minty fresh breath doesn't remedy the experience of exile that is common to humankind. No matter where we live, we find ourselves far from home. Author Jen Pollock Michel notes, "Home represents humanity's most visceral ache—and our oldest desire."[4]

This ancient desire is at the heart of our wandering. We are all people who live in exile, sent from Eden to make our way through a world shaped by sweat and sorrow. The state of exile is as familiar to us as our own heartbeat.

A little reflection can reveal just how pervasive this state of exile is. Where do you experience exile most acutely in your life?

For some of us, it's our family. Divorce, death, and dysfunction drive us from one another. Others recognize exile most clearly in our culture, as minority groups who've experienced systemic injustice and unholy discrimination find themselves on the outside looking in. Some of us find that the place that is supposed to be a community of love and welcome—our local church—has instead left us feeling like outcasts.

Each is a painful problem on its own. But at some level, these are symptoms pointing to the reality that our state of exile runs deep within each one of us. There is hopeful news, however. Exile is not a terminal point. It is not meant to be a destination.

Exile is meant to transform us into pilgrims.

The word "pilgrim" conjures images of unsmiling, black-garbed people who sailed to America on the *Mayflower*—or a lone backpacker with a walking stick, hiking to a distant holy site. While those capture the motion and intention of pilgrimage, the best image of a pilgrim is the one you see in the mirror when you're brushing your teeth with that minty fresh toothpaste.

Restlessness gets a bad rap in this world and can fan the flames of all kinds of sin. But it can also serve as a powerful compass. Fourth-century North African church father Augustine of Hippo famously prayed, "You have made us for yourself, and our hearts are restless, until they can find rest in you."[5]

Jesus highlighted how thoroughly He knew humanity's restless status when He told a religious leader inquiring about becoming His disciple, "Foxes have dens and birds have nests, but the Son of Man has no place to lay his head" (Matt. 8:20). Jesus wanted this man to know that following Him would uproot him from his settled, comfortable life. And that "settled-ness" is what passes for most of us as a salve for our state of exile.

Jesus is telling each one of us the same thing He told that man. He is calling us to un-settle and embrace a life of pilgrimage. He modeled it for us as He journeyed to the cross. Those who are settled and comfortable have no real incentive to follow Him. Nor are those who've wrapped themselves so firmly in the identity of exile they've learned to live in a bunker and sought salvation as a way of avoiding a world they don't particularly like. We who are a part of the church in the West have often framed discipleship in terms that speak to our craving for comfort or coach us to build better bunkers so we can avoid being contaminated by the sinful world around us.

The theme of pilgrimage runs through Scripture in three parallel, sometimes-overlapping streams:

- *Moral pilgrimage* focuses on everyday obedience to God.
- *Physical pilgrimage* emphasizes a bodily journey to a holy site in order to seek God.
- *Interior pilgrimage* describes the pursuit of communion with God through prayer, solitude, and contemplation.[6]

The book you hold in your hands will touch on all three as it traces the theme of pilgrimage from Genesis to Revelation.

It is time for us to reclaim our pilgrim identity. It is an identity for God's people woven through Scripture from beginning to end. This book will not only introduce you to the way in which the Bible highlights the pilgrim journey, but will help you recognize the invitations to pilgrimage God has placed in your life here and now. Each chapter ends with a few questions for contemplation or thoughtful conversation with a friend or small group, along with a pilgrim's prayer.

Author J. R. R. Tolkien rightly observed, "Not all those who wander are lost."

You were born—and born again—to wander.

CHAPTER 1

UPROOTED

Where are you from?

Most of us can answer the question with relative ease by naming the place we were born or perhaps the city where we spent our coming-of-age years.

It isn't quite so easy to answer a related question: Where are you going? We might be able to take a swat at it in the short-term ("to the kitchen to grab a snack"), but even those of us with excellent long-range forecasting skills know circumstances change. Plans need to be revised or scrubbed entirely.

I grew up in the northwest suburbs of Chicago during the 1960s and 1970s. There is a specificity to the time and place from which I launched. My family enjoyed deep-dish pizza. My sister and I watched the *Bozo the Clown* show on Channel 9 after walking home from school for lunch most every day. We shopped for back-to-school clothes at E. J. Korvette's in Niles. Those tidbits about my origins might explain some things about me, but they can't answer fully the question of where I'm from, nor are they the final word about where I'm going.

I was about sixteen and a new believer the first time I heard the phrase "God has a wonderful plan for your life." It was language I saw in evangelistic tracts and heard from a few well-meaning youth pastors. I imagined God had a specific set of instructions for me, and if I couldn't figure them out, it was an obvious failure of faith on my part. I pelted God with prayers that were thinly disguised demands: "Tell me where I am going, Lord. Really. I *need* to know." Those prayers were really anxious requests for God to download the cheat codes for my life into my soul so I could win (in His name, of course!) the game of adulthood. You probably won't be surprised to hear that He did not send me a wonderful plan for my life that included detailed career information, the name of my future spouse, the number of children I'd have, or the date I'd die.

This might tell you more about where I'm coming from than the tidbits about where my family shopped or the local television show I watched while I ate my lunchtime PB&J. My craving for an ironclad guarantee of success and safety is an expression of my culture's values as well as a peek inside the heart of a struggling teen teetering on the brink of independence.

"Where are you from? Where are you going?" Our individual life experiences are not sufficient to answer those Big Questions. And in a world that seems to warp in surreal ways at the speed of each day's headline, our time, place, and culture can't rightly interpret our past or guide us into our future. Attempting to ignore those questions leaves us as adrift as an empty plastic bottle floating on an unsettled sea.

But there is a powerful, true story that can rightly orient each one of us to where we've been and guide us onward. It isn't a new story, but revisiting it with those questions in mind can begin to help us understand the why behind our wandering.

WANDERING'S STARTING LINE

The origins for our status as wanderers are found in the first few pages of the Bible. Flip those tissue-thin pages open to Genesis 1, and you'll land in a perfect garden created to be a forever home for humankind. The man and woman who lived in this place led a peaceful existence free of the shadows of shame. The work they did to tend the place was so simple and joyful that it must have felt akin to what we call "play." Every meal in the garden was a feast shared in perfect communion and companionship with the One who spoke water droplets, bobcats, and pomegranates into being and said every atom of it was good.

Into the human ones He'd crafted to reflect His image, God wired the ultimate imprint of His love by giving them the holy freedom to choose whether they'd return His love. A single tree in the garden filled with groves of beautiful, fruit-filled trees was the test of this freedom and measure of their love. Would they do what their Creator was asking of them? This single Tree of Knowledge of Good and Evil carried with it one rule and a shattering consequence if Adam and Eve chose to violate that rule:

don't eat from this tree, because when you do, you will die (Gen. 2:16–17).

The Bible doesn't tell us how long the innocent pair stayed away from the tree. Days? Centuries? Yet humans know choice carries with it its own kind of hunger. The serpent smelled their hunger as if Adam and Eve were its prey. One twisted question from the scaly creature to Eve ("Did God really say . . . ?") drew woman and then man to sample fruit from the tree. Their choice to answer the serpent's question instead of responding in trust to God's declaration left them stripped bare of their innocence. They'd known good. Now they knew evil.

God followed through with the consequences He'd promised. He didn't destroy the world or abandon them. Instead, now armed with the knowledge of good and evil, humankind would discover the return route to communion with Him as they journeyed from Eden. One of the saddest images in Scripture is their final moment in the garden: "So the LORD God banished him from the Garden of Eden to work the ground from which he had been taken. After he drove the man out, he placed on the east side of the Garden of Eden cherubim and a flaming sword flashing back and forth to guard the way to the tree of life" (Gen. 3:23–24).

An instrument of death was used to guard the Tree of Life, the fiery sword brandished by angels is an image of holiness and judgment. As the exiled man and woman began walking away from Eden, they entered a world of struggle and second chances. There was no going back.

They were from Eden. But where were they going?

Genesis 4 records the first movements of the couple's new life outside the garden. Adam made love to his wife, and she bore him two sons. Delight mingled with exhaustion as Eve labored to bring children into the world, and Adam found the play he'd known in the garden become back-breaking hard work. Then they experienced the curse of death that cut straight to their hearts as their older son, Cain, murdered his younger brother, Abel. They lost Cain as God told him the consequences for his sin would be to spend the rest of his days living as a restless wanderer on the earth (Gen. 4:12).

Every subsequent generation was free to choose to respond in obedience to God, or not. Someone once told me that God has children, but no grandchildren. In other words, every generation must form their own fresh relationship with their heavenly Father. The faith their parents hold must become fully their own. The early generations of those exiled from Eden gradually disconnected from God, wandering so far that God spoke of putting an end to the world He made (Gen. 6:5–8).

Noah was born into this milieu. He was history's first countercultural rebel. His "rebellion" came in the form of walking faithfully with God when every single person around him was doing the opposite. This placed him solidly in the weirdo category to everyone in his world. His reputation probably suffered even more when he began building a boat the size of an ancient shopping mall after reporting to his neighbors that this is what God told him to do.

I wonder if he ever heard the whispered hiss of "Did God *really* say . . . ?" If he did, he silenced the whisper with his obedience, transforming his family's exile from Eden into a pilgrimage into the unknown.[1] Because of his faithfulness, you and I are here today (Heb. 11:7).

When Noah and his family disembarked from the ark after the flood waters receded, the ground was probably still sodden beneath their feet. God's delight-filled marching orders to the group echoed the command He gave to Adam at creation: be fruitful and multiply (Gen. 9:7). The group (and eventually, their descendants) embraced this command with gusto. Within a few generations, Noah's descendants realized all the multiplying they'd been doing would necessitate some division. There were simply too many people living in the same zip code.

Anxiety began breeding among the huddled masses living on the plain of Shinar. They didn't want to split up. The curse from Eden was more than hard work and painful childbirth. It was alienation. Isolation. Disconnection. The fear of the unknown— of being forgotten by one another and by God—birthed a plan among them that must have seemed like a certain solution to their problems: "Come, let us build ourselves a city, with a tower that reaches to the heavens, so that we may make a name for ourselves; otherwise we will be scattered over the face of the whole earth" (Gen. 11:4).

Blessing was embedded in God's command to Noah to multiply and increase. The fear gripping those descendants led them to misinterpret the blessing as a curse. They spoke the same language, so fear traveled at the speed of rumor through the people. Noah's descendants believed they'd suffer if they didn't take things into their own hands.

So they did just that. They'd lived as farmers and flock-herders to this point, but came together with the building program to end all building programs. They began work on a city—they were determined to stay together!—crowning it with a tower that would give them easy access to the God who seemed to live just beyond their grasp. The builders at Shinar may have used bricks to construct their city and tower, but they mortared them with a desire to control their destiny and their God.

As the Triune One surveyed the construction project at Shinar, He said, "If as one people speaking the same language they have begun to do this, then nothing they plan to do will be impossible for them. Come, let us go down and confuse their language so they will not understand each other" (Gen. 11:6–7).

In an instant, sonic dissonance whirled and divided the people. They splintered into dozens of ad hoc tribes, formed out of those who understood one another's frantic cries for help amid the cacophony of brand-new mother tongues.

It wasn't just the words that became confused in this chaos, but the meanings of the words. Does "dog" denote a Chihuahua or a Great Dane? When I say something is "interesting," does it mean it is truly fascinating or is it a catchall word to use when I don't know what else to say but want to keep the conversation moving?

Misunderstanding leads to confusion. And confusion leads to scattering. Both the tower built to access heaven and the event that sent the people into exile from one another are known as Babel, a name rooted in a word that means "to jumble."

In the sonic violence of the scattering at Shinar, it is a temptation to misinterpret not only words, but the very character of

God. Extract His love from the story, and Babel reads like the account of a capricious deity at play, watching humankind writhe and run like lab rats in a giant cosmic experiment.

But that is not who God is. The launch from Babel was meant to preserve His people, not destroy them. He gave polyglot tongues to them as a preservative as well as consequence. In perfect love, God intentionally disoriented them, sending them into exile from one another in order to reorient them to Himself. He'd made each one of them and knew they'd be able to hear His voice without translation through the noise as they began walking away from Shinar.

A MOVING TARGET

The accounts populating the first pages in our Bibles are at the heart of our human experience. Each of us knows the sorrow that comes from being disconnected from God and others.

A few years ago, my husband and I served as foster parents for a series of newborns. We considered opening our home to include older children in the foster system. I remember reading through a book published by our state featuring the descriptions of foster children waiting for adoption. These descriptions included lots of positive language about each child ("Michael is an affectionate eight-year-old who loves sports and video games") along with notes about any physical or mental health diagnoses the child had received.

I was struck by the fact that many of the children were being medicated for treatment of Attention Deficit/Hyperactivity

Disorder (ADHD). The diagnosis is used to describe a child who consistently has difficulty attending to and completing developmental-stage appropriate tasks like chores or school work. They can be impulsive and are often a bundle of nonstop, unfocused activity. I told a social worker friend I was a little startled by the high percentage of kids in the foster care system with this diagnosis.

She responded, "It's hard for grief to hit a moving target." She went on to explain that by the time a child ends up in foster care, they've almost always experienced an incredible amount of disruption, trauma, and loss. The ADHD diagnosis is, for a fair percentage of these children, both a result of their past losses and a coping mechanism for an uncertain present.

In varying degrees, we humans live as moving targets, trying to escape the existential grief of separation from God and others. This reality is at the heart of our wandering. Even those of us with relatively healthy family stories still experience the painful disconnect that comes from exile from Eden and the miscommunication that replays the Babel story in our lives on a regular basis.

One of the big questions of life is "Who am I?" Some suggest we find the answer to that question via the physical: our appearance, our gender. Some contend that identity resides in our ethnicity, network of relationships, or culture. Others say our identity is formed by what we do. This includes our work, our earning potential, even our hobbies and passions. Ethics defines identity for yet another group. We are defined by which moral choices we embrace and which we eschew.

Our sense of self takes a beating when we experience failure or face the severing of a meaningful relationship. We are disoriented when we lose our jobs or our kids leave the nest. Our souls are fragmented by the physical, cultural, economic, and ethical mirrors we use to define ourselves because those mirrors are not accurate. While those externals can provide helpful clues to the question of who we are, they are not reliable reflectors of truth.

We are more than just the sum of our own life experiences. We also carry within us the exile history of our forebears.

I am a Jewish follower of Jesus. My people, the Jews, have been wanderers for a very long time. We've lived far from home throughout most of our history, dispersed among the nations of the world yet preserved as a people.[2] We've faced the Inquisition, waves of persecution, expulsion en masse from various countries, the pogroms in Russia, and the Holocaust. In a 1996 speech, then-President of Israel, Ezer Weizman, said, "I am a wandering Jew who follows in the footsteps of my forebearers. And just as I escort them there and now and then, so do my forebearers accompany me and stand with me here today."[3] To live as a member of a diaspora community means you are a part of a people group scattered from their ancient homeland. My people have been imprinted—perhaps all the way down to the cellular level—by generations of terror and trauma, by our diaspora experience.

I wasn't surprised to learn that scientists have discovered that the effect of one generation's trauma may well be transmitted genetically to subsequent generations. This relatively new (and somewhat controversial) field of study is called epigenetics, which means, literally, "above the gene." Epigenetics researchers note that trauma changes the chemical structure surrounding our DNA. One generation's experience of suffering can be transmitted genetically to successive generations, heightening and intensifying physiological responses those descendants have to trauma and stress. The focus of current studies in this area include the descendants of Holocaust survivors and members of the Native American community, which also has a long history of generational trauma.[4]

Not long ago, I heard a hint of the way this generational experience of wandering can impact us. After my young adult son moved from the Midwest to Colorado, I asked him if he was homesick. Jacob told me he didn't feel he had the ability to miss a specific place. "I miss my family, but what I know how to do best is to keep moving." He had only two homes during his growing-up years, but he has generations of diaspora experience wired into his DNA. It's hard for grief to hit a moving target. He knows how to wander.

We all do. There is something familiar to every human being about the distress of damaged relationships, the disorientation of relocation, and the soul-altering grief of loss. The things in this world that mark us as wanderers point to our exile from Eden and scattering from Babel. They leave us with a sense of homesickness that not even the coziest home or the most joyous family reunion can ever dispel.

Author Stephen King said, "Homesickness is not always a vague, nostalgic, almost beautiful emotion, although that is somehow the way we always seem to picture it in our mind. It can be a terribly keen blade, not just a sickness in metaphor but in fact as well. It can change the way one looks at the world; the faces one sees in the street look not just indifferent but ugly . . .

perhaps even malignant. Homesickness is a real sickness—the ache of the uprooted plant."[5]

The ache of the uprooted plant is why we wander. We are born seekers. Curiosity and longing are at the core of who we are as human beings. We see curiosity in the 27,493 questions a day a three-year-old seems to ask. We can tap into longing as we cherish a nostalgic view of the past, hoping against hope that the good ol' days will salve the ache of our uprooted-ness.

But the ache of the uprooted plant is designed to graft us to the One who made us. Uprooted-ness is an uncomfortable identity and not one most of us would choose for ourselves.

Early church fathers said the state of humankind was that of the *homo viator* (traveler, pilgrim). We have been born to wander. The questions of where we're from or where we're going are clarified by this truth. They become: "Are we moving toward God or wandering away from him?"[6]

It is an unsettling question. Those who crave nostalgia or long to live in bunkers of contentment may not be interested in answering it. But for wanderers, the question is a reminder that exile has a purpose that goes far beyond telling us what our next zip code is to be.

To consider

1. In what ways would you say that wandering has marked your life so far? Your answer can include geographical wandering, but may also include relational scattering, vocational upheaval, or other kinds of disruption that led you away from where you thought you were going. How have these changes affected your life? Your faith?

2. As you reflect on the accounts shared here about the events detailed in the first few chapters of Scripture, what questions do you have regarding our status as wanderers? How do they connect with your own experience? Consider writing those questions in the form of a prayer or letter to God.

3. How have you seen the statement "It's hard for grief to hit a moving target" play out in your life?

_____

_____

_____

_____

_____

_____

_____

_____

_____

_____

_____

_____

_____

To pray

You who spoke the world into being by Your word, I honor You. You alone are God. There is no other.

In perfect, holy love, You made this world. In perfect, holy love, You embedded in humankind the ability to choose. In perfect, holy love, You have both preserved and corrected us even when we've chosen not to return Your love with our obedience. I grieve over all that has been damaged and savaged in this world. And I recognize the generational brokenness I carry and the weight of my own sin, both of which reside within me.

As I name my sin, Lord, I recognize something else just a little more clearly too. I recognize that I am a wanderer, longing to hide. I am an exile, living far from who You created me to be.

King David, who knew well his own brokenness, penned these words:

> Where can I go from your Spirit?
>> Where can I flee from your presence?
> If I go up to the heavens, you are there;
>> if I make my bed in the depths, you are there.
> If I rise on the wings of the dawn,
>> if I settle on the far side of the sea,
> even there your hand will guide me,
>> your right hand will hold me fast.
> If I say, "Surely the darkness will hide me
>> and the light become night around me,"

> even the darkness will not be dark to you;
>> the night will shine like the day,
>> for darkness is as light to you. (Ps. 139:7–12)

I cannot hide from You, though my sin makes me want to flee from You. Though I wander, there is nowhere I can go where You are not present. I am an exile, but that is not who You created me to be. As I pray these words in the name of the Father, Son, and Holy Spirit, I recognize that the questions of where I'm from and where I'm going are wrapped within my deep longing to journey with You.

Amen.

CHAPTER 2

SENT

Years ago, my husband and I got together with two other couples for dinner and an extended time of prayer on Friday evenings. Our children, a total of eight preschool and elementary-age kids, joined us for the meal and a short time of worship before heading off to play (and occasionally, to get into spats over Lego building projects) while we grown-ups prayed together.

One of the couples, Dan and Tracy, had grown increasingly restless. "We believe God wants us to share His love with Muslims. We know He's sending us ... somewhere."

In the church all three families attended, there was no higher calling than that of a cross-cultural missionary. Though we'd all heard that calling valorized from the pulpit, we'd also seen a couple of disastrous results as a starry-eyed young adult boarded a plane to go preach the gospel on the other side of the world, only to return home a couple of years later broken by the challenge of being a cultural outsider.

Dan and Tracy harbored no such idealistic notions. They'd been intentional about preparing themselves to go. They'd paid off their debts. Dan had pursued completion of his college degree. They chose to live in a gang-infested neighborhood in a tiny old two-flat, renting out the upstairs apartment so they could live carefully within their limited means. They'd invested much of their free time in cross-cultural ministry, serving as English language tutors for dozens of Muslim immigrants. And the pair sought every opportunity to be mentored by other long-term missionaries.

We could all feel the pressure building in them as they waited and waited for God's green light. Tracy once said half-jokingly, "I told Dan maybe each person in our family should pack a suitcase, then we'll go to the airport and wait there until God tells us which plane to get on."

When God did make it clear where they were supposed to go next, they didn't need a plane to get there. They relocated about thirty miles away when they were invited to help launch a storefront ministry center in a city neighborhood with a large immigrant Hindu and Muslim population. For the next two decades, they were involved full time in outreach to their neighbors—neighbors who often became friends—as they facilitated English language conversation groups and kids' clubs and spearheaded a ministry to cab drivers. Sounds like a happy resolution for Dan and Tracy, doesn't it?

But this was not the end of their story. It turned out they'd need those suitcases after all.

GO . . . SOMEWHERE?

Unlike Dan and Tracy, nearly four thousand years ago, Abram had no dreams of going anywhere. His extended family lived in Ur, located in what is now southern Iraq. The land's bounty sustained the family herds, owing to its location near the junction of the Tigris and Euphrates Rivers.

Scripture doesn't give us much of a backstory for Abram, to whom we're introduced in Genesis 12 when he's seventy-five years old. We do learn elsewhere in Scripture that Abram's father Terah served other gods (Josh. 24:2). Genesis 12 also introduces us to Abram's wife, Sarai. The couple is childless, an issue of deep shame and sorrow in their culture. Yet Abram is a one-woman man. He has taken no other wives so he can get himself an heir. In short, they are living a pretty standard exile's existence.

Scripture doesn't tell us whether Abram was seeking the one true God. But we discover that God was seeking him:

> The Lord had said to Abram, "Go from your country, your people and your father's household to the land I will show you. I will make you into a great nation, and I will bless you; I will make your name great, and you will be a blessing. I will bless those who bless you, and whoever curses you I will curse; and all peoples on earth will be blessed through you." (Gen. 12:1–3)

God spoke to Abram in the imperative. The Hebrew words *lech lecha* used here for the command "go" emphasize this wasn't a casual suggestion. *Lech*, which is pronounced with the guttural "ch" sound used in the word "Chanukah," means "walk" and "come" in addition to "go."[1] *Lecha* is a preposition that means to, toward, or for, and gives intensity and direction to the "go." Rabbi Jeff Goldwasser suggests the words "Abram, get yourself going!" offers a fair modern paraphrase of *lech lecha*.[2]

Lech lecha has big implications for wanderers. "Go" is a word that changes things. It puts an end to inertia: Rise thou from thine La-Z-Boy! Lech lecha also carries the answer to the "How?" and "Where?" questions that follow in the immediate wake of "Go."

How? By walking.

Where? Toward the One who bids you to come.

Lech lecha tells us the Lord is our launchpad. He is our companion on the way. And He is our destination. Lech lecha is the road map for the pilgrim's journey.

As Abram learned, this "map" reads like a blank piece of paper. Reflecting on Abram, one commentator noted, "Knowing where one is going gives a person a sense of autonomy and control over his life . . . By freely giving up our autonomy and control, we become, in effect, instruments to realize the will of God in this world."[3] There was no logical reason Abram should have considered wandering from the security of his home and extended family at age seventy-five. However, as Abram surrendered to God, he found himself free to realize the will of God in this world. Lech lecha, Abram.

God's call to Abram had promises attached. God would give him a place. God would make from him a people. Abram's descendants would become a conduit of God's blessing for the rest of the world.

The promises were conditional on Abram's obedience. Scripture offers only a couple of tantalizing clues about why this aging, barren son of an idolater was chosen by God. Abram's forebear, Noah, is said to have walked with God (Gen. 6:9). In the final movement of Abram's life, Abram used similar language to describe his own long journey with God: ". . . the LORD, before whom I have walked faithfully" (Gen. 24:40). This language hints that perhaps Abram had begun his journey to seek the one true God long before he'd taken a single step.

In any case, God spoke. And Abram went. A popular saying about pilgrimage is, "We make the road by walking." It is true that where there is no road, the only way we discern the next step is to put one foot in front of the other. We are not our own GPS, however. God's lech lecha tells us He is going with us. Abram's story shows that we do not wander in vain, nor do we journey alone.

I can't imagine what the parting was like as Abram, his wife (and half-sister) Sarai (Gen. 20:12), his nephew Lot, and their bond-servants left the security of their father's house to take the first steps into the unknown. Did everyone else in their family celebrate? Did they pepper him with questions about this open-ended assignment from a God they couldn't see? Why did Lot elect to accompany his uncle while other family members stayed behind? Did any of those traveling with him ever second-guess the decision to go?

Did Abram?

The group and their herds traveled four hundred to six hundred miles across the Fertile Crescent before entering the land of Canaan. There was no welcoming committee to greet them. Other people lived in the land God had revealed to Abram as his destination. The pilgrims pitched their tents first in the region of Canaan known as Shechem, and the Lord appeared to Abram and repeated the promise to the homeless, old, childless man that Abram's descendants would possess the land.

In response, Abram built an altar to the Lord there. He worshiped the one true God in the midst of the idol-worshiping Canaanite people. He then traveled southward, stopping in the hammock of land between the Canaanite cities of Bethel and Ai to build another altar to the Lord. Genesis 12:8 says in this location he called on the name of the Lord. The Hebrew word *qara*, or "call," used in this passage means proclaiming, hounding, or crying out. Abram's "altar call" was loud, persistent, and evangelistic.

The Bible reports that a famine in Canaan eventually drove Abram and company south into Egypt. Abram may have been tempted to pitch his tents there, choosing a life in exile from Ur over the discomforting existence of a spiritual nomad. Even when he wandered to the shady side of the truth and handed his wife over to another man in Egypt so he could save his own skin, he had not been able to wander beyond the unbreakable promise of God.

Sometime after Abram made his way back to Canaan, God cemented the earlier call He'd given to Abram in the form of a formal, permanent covenant. God came to Abram in a vision. He told Abram He was Abram's defender and provision. In response, Abram asked the questions burning in his soul: Who will inherit all You have provided for me? How will I ever possess this land when others live here (Gen. 15:1–8)?

In our culture, we think of contracts, or covenants, as something brokered between lawyers—and contracts always have loopholes, because we have loopholes in our souls.

God has no loopholes. There is no Plan B with Him. God sealed His commitment to Abram and Abram's descendants with language Abram would understand. We are used to contracts printed on paper, so when we read Genesis 15, we may recoil at the image of cutting animals in half and walking between them as a way of sealing the deal, but it was a way people in the ancient Near East communicated the whole-life, deadly seriousness of a covenant. Everyone clearly understood that if either party broke the promise, the violator would face the same end the animal did.

In this case, it was the presence of God alone who moved through those bleeding carcasses. As God enacts the covenant, He tells Abram he will live to a ripe old age, but his descendants will be enslaved for four hundred years in a land not their own before they fully possess the land He's promised to Abram (Gen. 15:12–21).

After God makes His covenant with Abram, Sarai comes up with the idea of bringing God's promise to fruition at last by using her Egyptian maid Hagar as her surrogate. It is a way she can affirm what Abram has experienced with his God. Out of this arrangement, Abram receives a son. He names him Ishmael, which means "God listens." This beautiful boy must have seemed for all the world like he was the answer to Abram's prayers.

Thirteen years pass, and Ishmael is at the brink of manhood when God once again visits sojourner Abram, now ninety-nine years old. This time, God reiterates His covenant promises and speaks a change of identity to both Abram and Sarai. Abram means "exalted father," which must have been his own father's prayer for Abram when he gave Abram that name. God changed his name to Abraham, which means "father of many." Sarai, whose name meant "my princess," became simply Sarah—princess, a name befitting her role as matriarch of a family who'd become as numerous as the stars in the sky. In this visitation, God told Abram every male in his household would need to make a cut in the most private part of their anatomy so they could mark themselves as children of the covenant. Circumcision would be a daily reminder to his offspring that they were born into relationship with God.

God's visitation, followed by another divine encounter confirming the promise of a son led the aging couple together to seek God intimately (Gen. 18:1–18). One year after his own circumcision, one-hundred-year-old Abraham and his nonagenarian wife Sarah became parents of Isaac, just as God promised (Gen. 21:1–7). Lech lecha.

WALK WITH ME

"Follow me." When Jesus said these words, they bore the same meaning as lech lecha. Come to Me. Leave your old way of life. Walk with Me.

Jesus called Simon and his brother Andrew with these words. They came from a family of basic working-class guys, plying their trade as freshwater fishermen on the Sea of Galilee. Jesus spotted Simon and Andrew and used the imperative to open the conversation: "Follow me" (Matt. 4:18–20; Luke 5:1–11; John 1:40–42).

No long period of deliberation is recorded here. Jesus called. They followed.

Jesus chose the Aramaic form of Simon's name, Peter, to use for him at the start of their life together on the road. Peter—*petros*—means "pebble or small rock."[4] Despite his sometimes clumsy pilgrimage following Jesus during the years of Jesus' earthly ministry, Peter is given a new identity by Jesus as he journeys with Him.

They'd been together for some time when Jesus asks His disciples who people think He is. They chorus a variety of responses: John the baptizer, Elijah, Jeremiah, one of the other prophets (Matt. 16:14). Jesus then asks them who they say He is. Peter's answer was pure revelation from God: "You are the Messiah, the Son of the living God" (Matt. 16:16).

In this sacred moment, Jesus names Peter's true identity: "You are Peter (*petros*) and on this rock (*petra*) I will build my church" (Matt. 16:18). Jesus uses a play on words here to tell Peter he is not a pebble, but bedrock, an immovable boulder, a foundation who will be used to build the community of living stones—the church (1 Peter 2:5).

LOOKING FOR ME
IN ALL THE WRONG PLACES

I hear well-meaning Christian speakers encouraging their audiences to "Discover your destiny!", "Pursue your dreams!", or

"Claim your promises!" This slogan-based approach to faith mixes a bit of Scripture with our desires for fame, fortune, and our own piece of the American Dream, and it doesn't look much like the kind of journey Jesus had in mind for His followers.

This pursuit of worldly success, baptized in Bible-sounding language, sadly passes in many quarters for teaching about how to understand our identity in Christ. This kind of self-focused ambition is little more than a sparkly version of exile.

There was no fame-and-fortune bait on the hook when Jesus told Peter He'd make him a fisher of men. There was no promise of celebrity when God spoke to Abram and told him to leave the comfort of home and family. Both men's lives—and the lives of most others highlighted in the Bible—became less comfortable and far more uncertain after God called them.

Lech lecha. Follow Me. This is how we learn our true identity.

Jesus put the emphasis on followership when He said, "Whoever wants to be my disciple must deny themselves and take up their cross and follow me" (Matt. 16:24). Who we were meant to be is revealed only as we learn to follow. Those steps away from our regularly-scheduled ideas of what our life is supposed to look like uproot us from our state of exile. They pivot us toward pilgrimage. It is on that very journey into the unknown that Abram became Abraham and Simon became Peter. It is how we will become most truly ourselves.

Danish philosopher Søren Kierkegaard said:

> They call themselves *believers* and thereby signify that they
> are pilgrims, strangers, and aliens in the world. Indeed, a
> staff in the hand does not identify a pilgrim ... as definitely

as calling oneself a believer publicly testifies that one is on a journey, because faith simply means: What I am seeking is not here, and for that very reason I believe it. Faith expressly signifies the deep, strong, blessed restlessness that drives the believer so that he cannot settle down at rest in this world, and therefore the person who has settled down completely at rest has also ceased to be a believer, because a believer cannot sit still as one sits with a pilgrim's staff in one's hand—a believer travels forward.[5]

Dan and Tracy, our old friends who ached to jump on a plane and head to another country to be missionaries, ended up spending two decades following God as they served faithfully in that storefront ministry center. Then, when they were least expecting it, they heard it: "Lech lecha. It's time to go."

They sold most everything they had, packed those suitcases, and finally got on that plane. They've spent the last few years in the Middle East, caring for refugees and exiles in the name of Jesus.

Living with the "deep, strong, blessed restlessness" of the pilgrim can be an uncomfortable way to live. But it is far better than the alternative.

To consider

1. The way in which Abram and Simon were called is direct and dramatic. Does it always work that way? Why or why not?

2. God did not give Abram a road map for his journey from Ur. Are there areas in your life for which you're longing for clear direction from Him? What is most worrisome or confusing for you about not knowing precisely where you're going?

3. What influences have shaped your notions of who you are supposed to be?

_____
_____
_____
_____
_____
_____
_____
_____
_____
_____
_____
_____
_____
_____
_____
_____
_____
_____

To pray

Here I am, Lord.

I may not have a dramatic story of Your calling me like Abram or Simon had. But I am here, in conversation with You, precisely because You have called me. Jesus, You told Your followers "No one comes to me unless the Father who sent me draws them" (John 6:44). Even this prayer is a response to Your calling of me.

I don't know where I'm going. But I do know You've asked me to follow You. To leave my old way of life. And to walk with You into the unknown of today.

I pray these words for this day: "Let the morning bring me word of your unfailing love, for I have put my trust in you. Show me the way I should go, for to you I entrust my life" (Ps. 143:8). Holy Spirit, please teach me how I am to respond to Your lech lecha today.

In the name of the One who said, "Follow Me," I pray. Amen.

CHAPTER 3

WAYLAID

Contentment can be a gift. A pillow and soft bed for a road-weary soul.

Or it can be a velvet-covered trap.

In the face of a famine that transformed the arid soil of Canaan into gritty dust, Jacob's family of tumbleweed nomads put on hold their dreams of settling down in a forever home. The specter of starvation required decisive action, or else there wouldn't be anyone left to carry on the legacy of the promise given by God to his grandfather Abraham. The promise was a treasure, but it seemed to be more theoretical than practical in the face of a drought. Contentment is a pie-in-the-sky luxury when there's no food. And you can't eat a promise.

There was precedent in this family for doing what they needed to do to survive. Jacob's grandfather, Abraham, had to leave this very same land so he could take refuge in Egypt amidst a famine during his lifetime (Gen. 12:10–20). Out of ideas and low on food, Jacob elected to send ten of his sons to travel to Egypt to buy grain, then return to him (Gen. 42:1–38). He might as well have torn out his own already-broken heart to send with them on their journey southward. He'd been grieving the death of his favored son Joseph for years and was loathe to launch most of his other children on a dangerous ten-day trek to Egypt, but there was safety in numbers when it came to travel.[1] All of them would surely die if he didn't send someone to Egypt for provisions.

This decision seems to support what the trusty Psychology 101 standard, Maslow's Hierarchy of Needs, describes about human behavior. Psychologist Abraham Maslow's pyramid-shaped diagram illustrates how humans prioritize needs, describing the way in which we first must address our urgent physical requirements for food, clothing, shelter, and safety before we're free to focus on other higher-level desires such as building relationships or focusing on creative tasks. According to Maslow, when every need is met, we will be self-actualized: we will become all we can be.

While this "be all you can be" business sounds like the stuff of contemporary pep rallies and self-esteem workshops, we do well to remember that those of us living in twenty-first-century Western culture live in privileged space. We have the freedom to pursue some of those higher-level desires described by Dr. Maslow. The fact that you're holding this book in your hands means you have enough cushion in your life to sit and read rather than trying to figure out where your next meal is coming from.

When Jacob sent ten of his sons to Egypt in search of food,

the story had a stunning twist. He never would have imagined that his family's hunger would lead him back to the thing he hungered for most—his son Joseph. Years earlier, with a performance of sorrow that would have won the lot of them an ancient version of an Academy Award, Jacob's other sons told their father that their brother, his petted, coddled son Joseph, had been lost to a wild animal's ravening hunger. Instead, they'd plotted to rid their family of him. They'd sold him into slavery.

When they got to Egypt, they discovered their long-lost brother was alive and thriving.

After the shock and awe of the revelation, the family was reunited and restored. They added this miraculous new chapter to their family's story. As they did, they unpacked their suitcases and parked themselves in the comfort of upper-caste Egyptian society, thanks to Joseph's role as second-in-command of the land. No need to rush back to Canaan when there was no food anyway. Being together was the main thing. Being together in the comfort of Pharaoh's court made it easier to extend their stay.

The first hint that going home might not be so simple came when the family sought to honor Jacob's final wish that he be buried in the same place where his wife, parents, and grandparents rested (Gen. 49:29–32). Joseph sought permission from his boss, Pharaoh, to carry his father's body to Canaan.

Pharaoh went him one better. He sent pretty much his entire government to Canaan, including a military accompaniment, along with Joseph's brothers and all the adult members of their households. The entire company spent seven days in mourning near the Jordan River, then proceeded to Canaan for the burial (Gen. 50:1–14). Scripture ends the account of the journey with these spare words: "After burying his father, Joseph returned to Egypt, together with his brothers and all the others who had gone with him to bury his father" (Gen. 50:14). This must have seemed at the time like incredible favor to have this kind of escort. But something in these words tells me the family moved into a velvet cage upon their return.

What was the moment Jacob's children realized they couldn't go home? When did they figure out they were no longer guests, but prisoners?

Scripture is silent on when and how the people became slaves. All we know is that at some point, time passed, Joseph and his generation died out, and the leadership of Egypt changed hands a few times. Joseph's history of distinguished service became a footnote in another leader's reign (Ex. 1:8–10).

When Joseph was alive, his supernatural gift of dream interpretation and his skill at strategic thinking led Pharaoh to give him the position of governing all the economic affairs of Egypt (Gen. 41). During the years when drought affected both Canaan and Egypt, in his role as second-in-command in Egypt, Joseph purchased thousands of acres of Egyptian land and pressed the people into slavery:

> So Joseph bought all the land in Egypt for Pharaoh. The Egyptians, one and all, sold their fields, because the famine was too severe for them. The land became Pharaoh's, and Joseph

reduced the people to servitude, from one end of Egypt to the other....

Joseph said to the people, "Now that I have bought you and your land today for Pharaoh, here is seed for you so you can plant the ground. But when the crop comes in, give a fifth of it to Pharaoh. The other four-fifths you may keep as seed for the fields and as food for yourselves and your households and your children." (Gen. 47:20–21, 23–24)

I've wondered if this practice laid the groundwork for what trapped Joseph's descendants in Egypt a few generations later.

When I read about how some lower-caste families in India today have been enslaved for generations to pay off an ancestor's debt—a debt that can never be repaid because the system is rigged against them—I can imagine something like this may have happened to the descendants of the seventy people who came from Canaan in search of food. The international advocacy organization Free the Slaves describes the process by which a family becomes ensnared permanently in the slavery of debt bondage:

In debt bondage, slaves are chained to an illegal financial obligation that they are forced to repay through endless labor. If unrelenting psychological pressure fails, slave holders enforce their grip through direct violence. The crushing mechanisms of bonded labor slavery are insidious, humiliating, and powerful. An entire family—men, women, and children—is forced to work for the person who holds the debt. If a slave gets sick and misses work, the debt grows. Slaves are paid only enough to stay alive to work another day. Usurious interest rates ensure they can never earn enough to repay the debt. Those in slavery cannot walk away, even if they could pay off the loan more quickly by working elsewhere. Debt bondage has been outlawed in India, but impoverished villagers do not know their rights—and many have no choice but to borrow funds when a family emergency arises.[2]

As I read about this practice, I grieve for those who've been trapped in this cycle for years. I wonder how many generations it takes a family to forget the amount of the original debt, the figure buried under years of sweat and sorrow. I wonder how long it takes for them to forget they ever had a life of their own.

THREE GENERATIONS?

My own family's recent history has shown me it doesn't take many years for one generation's experience to become little more than a footnote in the story of subsequent generations. My paternal grandmother, Leah Cohen, grew up in the Pale of Settlement in Russia. This region was a giant, mostly rural Jewish ghetto that existed from the late 1700s until the Russian Revolution in 1917. On modern maps, this region included parts of Lithuania, Belarus, Ukraine, Moldova, Poland, Latvia, and a swath of western Russia.[3]

Though things were never easy for the people who scratched out an existence from the land, by the start of the twentieth century, intensifying persecution from the Russian government and waves of massacres of defenseless Jewish villages led to a flood of people seeking to leave the area. The number one dream destination for families was America, where it was rumored that the streets were paved with gold. Leah arrived at Ellis Island in the early 1920s and never looked back.

A couple of her family members had already made their way to central Illinois, and she followed them there. Shortly after arriving, Leah and one of her siblings married another set of siblings. Leah and husband, Jake, had one son, and the little family sought to balance their identity as Jews while at the same time seeking to not stand out among their Gentile neighbors—not an easy task in the thirties and forties, when anti-Semitism in America was on the rise.

The horrors of life in Russia and across Eastern Europe resurfaced among the Jewish community in America as revelations hit the headlines in the wake of World War II about what Adolph Hitler and the Nazis had done to six million Jewish people. The horrors of Stalin's brutal regime in the Soviet Union trickled into the press as well, and underscored for my grandmother that she'd gotten out of the Old Country in the nick of time.

My grandmother never spoke of Russia to her son, nor to my sister and me, her two granddaughters. I remember asking her once about her life in the Old Country after my first viewing of *Fiddler on the Roof.* The movie highlights what life was like in the Pale of Settlement and presents a scrubbed, Hollywood version of a pogrom, complete with Broadway show tunes. In response to my query, Grandma Leah waved her hand in front of her face like she was swatting away a swarm of bees and said, "You don't want to talk about it," which was her way of saying she didn't want to talk about it. Ever. The past was a memory locked in the vault of my grandmother's heart.

Author Warsan Shire said of her Somali family's more recent

flight to the U.K., "No one leaves home unless home is the mouth of a shark."[4] For my grandmother, Russia was the mouth of a shark, and those gleaming teeth had grazed a little too close for her comfort. To the best of my knowledge, my grandmother never expressed a moment of longing for her childhood home, likely because she didn't have a drop of nostalgia for the fear, privation, and hunger she experienced there. Though she lived as a minority in the majority, corn-fed Bible Belt–culture of central Illinois, and was on the receiving end of anti-Semitic comments and treatment throughout her life, it seemed she consoled herself with the fact that at least Peoria wasn't Russia.

When I thought about how quickly Russia became a distant memory in my family story as my grandmother sunk her roots into rich American soil, I began to understand how easily Jacob's descendants could have transplanted their rootless roots into the soil of Egypt. No one wants to be poor or hungry.

Though Jacob's children knew the stories of their family's past and the shining beauty of God's promise to them for the future, the gravitational pull of comfort and a full belly anchored them in Egypt. Going home to Canaan became a memory instead of a prayer.

When Jacob brought his family down to Egypt, his people had lived in Canaan for less than three generations, totaling perhaps two hundred years at most. Before that, they'd been wanderers. Rootlessness had formed their identity before God had called them into irrevocable relationship with him.

And none of this was a surprise. When God was initiating His covenant relationship with Abraham, He gave Abraham a sneak peek of what was to come:

> "Know for certain that for four hundred years your descendants will be strangers in a country not their own and that they will be enslaved and mistreated there. But I will punish the nation they serve as slaves, and afterward they will come out with great possessions. You, however, will go to your ancestors in peace and be buried at a good old age. In the fourth generation your descendants will come back here, for the sin of the Amorites has not yet reached its full measure." (Gen. 15:13–16)

Jacob's children carried these holy words with them when they headed into Egypt to buy grain during the famine, but I suspect they didn't connect this prophecy to what they must have imagined was going to be a temporary pit stop. Empty bellies awaited them if they returned to Canaan too soon. Better to stay put and ride out the drought in comfort.

Sure, they were living in a land not their own. Yes, the children born there would always be aliens, marked by circumcision and held by God's covenant promises. Certainly, judgment would come to Egypt as well as to the idolatrous Amorite tribe who claimed Canaan as their own.

But all that would come later. Much later. For now, Abraham's grandson and his children just wanted somewhere to lay their heads.

UNPACKING

The desire to stop moving, unpack, and rest in a place of safety is a good one. In fact, the longing for security and protection is a second-tier desire on Maslow's Hierarchy of Needs. It explains why Jacob's children so readily nestled into Egypt's comforts. It explains how they could have missed the early warning signs that they were no longer welcome guests.

In my own wanderings, I crave security too. I want to unpack my bags and stop moving. I want to know I'm sheltered and protected. I long to exhale, rest deeply, and be in one place long enough to "bloom where I'm planted." I long to experience the contentment that flows from knowing I am safe and secure.

I've spent more than four decades in suburban church culture, where I hear the word "contentment" used as sort of a mark of sacrifice in responding to consumer culture: "I wanted to remodel my kitchen, but God is helping me learn to be content with a new glass tile backsplash instead."

I've also heard contentment used as Christian-speak to simultaneously broadcast ambition while signaling the virtue of humility: "I believe I'm called to be in charge of women's ministries in this church someday, but right now, I am content teaching the toddler Sunday school class. Ooooh! I just love those kiddos!"

When Christians throw around the word contentment, I think of a favorite line delivered by Inigo Montoya, the sword-wielding anti-hero in the 1987 movie *The Princess Bride*: "You keep using that word. I do not think it means what you think it means."

First Timothy 6:6 tells us, "Godliness with contentment is

great gain." I suspect Paul, who penned these words to his young protégé, Timothy, would be very confused by the way in which we use "contentment." The Greek word *autarkeia* used for contentment in this verse means that a person is resting in a place of safety and security in their lives. The context for this verse is a discussion of the greed of false teachers and the lure of our own acquisitive desires. Godly contentment says "enough" instead of spouting Christianized versions of "I want more." I appreciate the irony of Paul saying that godly contentment is the only "more" for which we should be aiming.

Godly contentment will keep us in a state of discontentment with the world around us. It will help us recognize temporary comforts such as a full stomach and a safe place in which to lay our heads are not the destination in our lives. Godly contentment makes pilgrims out of us.

The kind of contentment that Jacob's children thought they'd found in Egypt didn't last.

When the curtain rises on the family several generations later in Exodus 1, safety and security were long gone for the people who'd carried the promise of God in their very DNA.

To consider

1. What do you know about your grandparents' lives? What questions do you wish you could ask them about their youth? Their joys? Their regrets? (If they are still alive, consider making it a point to ask them those questions while you still can!)

2. Have you ever had an experience where you found you were trapped in a situation or relationship from which it was difficult to extricate yourself? Were there warning signs you may have missed along the way? Has the situation been resolved?

3. What is your definition of contentment? How does it jive with the way in which contentment has been described in this chapter?

_____

_____

_____

_____

_____

_____

_____

_____

_____

_____

_____

To pray

Heavenly Father, I want to unpack my bags and be home. Because of that desire, there are times I've sought shortcuts so I can try to skip the scary, uncertain parts of the journey. At other points, I've grown impatient and sought to meet my needs in ways that seemed practical and clever, but weren't Your best for me. I've craved comfort and security, and I've labeled those cravings "contentment."

You placed the desire for home within me. You've wired me with needs for food and shelter and safety. And I recognize that sometimes, I've focused on meeting those needs in ways that have compromised me. Those compromises have led me further into exile, away from You. Please forgive me, and set me on the right path.

Your Word says, "Lead me, LORD, in your righteousness because of my enemies—make your way straight before me" (Ps. 5:8). My enemies may want to take my life, or they may simply want to woo me from You with false promises of security and comfort. Awaken me to the ways in which I've baptized the world's view of contentment in spiritual language.

Please, Jesus, help me accept Your gift of holy discontent as a way in which I will discover what it means to live as a pilgrim. How I want to follow You, Lord! Please guide me.

I ask these things in the name of the One who is the way, the truth, and the life.

Amen.

CHAPTER 4

DISPLACED

I'd written my own job description, and they gave me my own office. After volunteering regularly at a church I loved, I was invited to join the inner circle and become a paid staff member. My view from the inner circle was quite different than what I'd witnessed from the pews (okay, the padded stackable chairs). The leaders I admired from afar on Sundays were very different Monday through Friday. No one now or then would ever label me an idealist, but even with lots of tough life experience, I was caught unawares by these dynamics. After my clumsy attempts at trying to help the culture were rebuffed, I decided it best to resign from my position, just shy of my one-year anniversary in the role.

My exit from the job snipped the final frayed thread tying us to the town where we'd lived for several years. My husband and I knew staying at the church wasn't an option. Anyway, we'd never felt as though we'd transplanted into the community. Now that our nest was emptying, we wondered if it might be time to move on. We prayed and decided to test the water by listing the house. It sold the first day it hit the market.

We found a place to rent at the edge of a nearby metropolitan area while we tried to discern what was next for us. My husband commuted to his old job and spent nights and weekends looking for a new position in our new target area of "Somewhere Closer to Our Rental Property Probably." I expected to feel peace—or at least relief—at last now that the last several years were in the rearview mirror.

After the boxes were unpacked, I found a part-time job at a bookstore. As I squatted on the filthy carpet shelving books for minimum wage, I finally had a bit of space to feel some feelings after a whirlwind of adrenaline-fueled packing, moving, and goodbyes. I flipped through the pages of the book in my hand. At the back of the volume was a handful of blank pages.

It was a metaphor for our lives. Our future felt like a bunch of empty pages. While my former coworkers seemed to be comfortable with the status quo, I was sitting on the filthy floor, staring at mouse droppings littering the floor beneath the sagging bookshelves.

The blank pages left plenty of space for my questions: How could they get away with it? God, why did You let this happen to me? To my family?

I knew the theologically correct answers to my unanswerable questions: God was right here with me. And in His time, He would reveal what had been going on behind closed church doors. He would also reveal the sin that had been fermenting inside me regarding my responses to all that had happened during my time on staff.

Knowing the right answers did not bring me any comfort. I wrapped my heart in a husk of protective self-pity. I felt as though I'd been abandoned in the wilderness.

A counselor would have said I was experiencing normal grief that followed our abrupt relocation. We'd moved many times before. I recognized that grief. What I wasn't prepared for this time was the anesthetizing nature of self-pity, the drug I'd chosen to stanch the pain of disappointment in those who claimed to be my brothers and sisters in Jesus. John Gardner, the Secretary of Health, Education, and Welfare under President Lyndon Johnson, once said, "Self-pity is easily the most destructive of the non-pharmaceutical narcotics; it is addictive, gives momentary pleasure and separates the victim from reality."[1]

Poor old me was stuck in a mindless job, living in a rundown rental townhouse, with no idea what the next step would be. The information I'd learned about God through the years was scant comfort when it seemed so lonely and disorienting in that wilderness. Self-pity seemed to offer a safe, warm shelter from all those confusing questions.

Self-pity is the fruit of pride, which is the root of all other kinds of sin. My self-pity was rooted in a warped sense of my own importance ("How dare they treat me that way?") and flowered in envy ("I want the comfort and sense of belonging they seem to have") and anger ("How dare they treat me that way?"). Bishop Joseph Hall noted the isolating nature of self-pity: "The proud man hath no God; the envious man hath no neighbor; the angry man hath not himself. What good, then, in being a man, if one has neither himself nor a neighbor nor God?"[2]

When I asked, "Have you brought us here only to abandon us, God?," I thought I knew the answer.

At that point, I was pretty sure the answer might be yes.

WHY CRY IF THERE IS NO HOPE FOR HEARING?

Have you ever seen the epic 1956 Technicolor film *The Ten Commandments*? The movie gave us Charlton Heston as the penultimate Moses, a manly man with a full head of perfectly coiffed silvery hair, a giant white beard, and a deep bass voice. Nearly everyone in the movie spoke with that vaguely British movie accent so popular in movies made then except for Dathan, played by character actor Edward G. Robinson. Dathan sounded like a New York gangster. The movie's hypersaturated colors and cheesy special effects turned the story of Exodus 1–14 into a Technicolor fairy tale instead of a gritty true story marked with both incredible suffering and supernatural deliverance.

We get a sense of the story's reality when we invite our senses into our reading of the black and white text in our Bibles. If we read, "During that long period, the king of Egypt died. The Israelites groaned in their slavery and cried out, and their cry for help because of their slavery went up to God" (Ex. 2:23), it behooves us to stop and smell the sweat, see the sight of the whip tearing back flesh, and hear the sound of curses meant to further dehumanize the enslaved children of Israel. If we tune our ears to listen a little closer amidst the cacophony, we'll catch the cry of an eight-day-old Hebrew baby boy as a knife marks him for life through circumcision as a son of Abraham.

The moans of the exiles who'd become slaves were a wordless plea to God for release. Theologian Martin Marty noted, "Even the cry from the depths is an affirmation: Why cry if there is no hint of hope of hearing?"[3]

God heard them loud and clear. He sent a deliverer to His people who knew the language of the Egyptian court, the isolation that came from running into the desert to hide, and the interruption of the eternal God breaking into an ordinary day. Moses went to see Pharaoh in order to request that his enslaved people be permitted to head into the desert for three days to worship God (Ex. 5:1–3). Pharaoh refused, and God used Moses to announce a series of ten plagues that would afflict the Egyptian people. Each of those ten afflictions was a direct confrontation by the one true God with the pantheon of faux gods of Egypt.[4]

The day Pharaoh released the Chosen People was a demonstration of God's power to them as He parted the waters of the sea, allowing them to pass. It also revealed the darkness of Pharaoh's heart as he reversed his decision and sent his army in pursuit of the slaves he'd freed hours earlier. Pharaoh's choice was a costly one, as his army perished when the sea flooded back into its normal footprint (Ex. 14:26–30).

Day one of freedom for the Hebrew people ended well: "And when the Israelites saw the mighty hand of the LORD displayed against the Egyptians, the people feared the LORD and put their trust in him and in Moses his servant" (Ex. 14:31).

A couple of days later, the rosy glow had faded. They'd journeyed three days into the hot, dry desert and their physical thirst overtook their hunger for freedom. It takes about three days without water to die a painful death from dehydration. It is worth noting that way back before all the plagues hit, three days was the amount of time Moses requested of Pharaoh so the Hebrew slaves could head into the desert to worship. Moses had first asked the man in whose household he'd been raised for a three-day respite from slavery for his people (Ex. 5:1–5).

Enslavement had gotten the Hebrew people in the habit of seeing themselves in terms of what they were lacking. Lack of food had brought them to Egypt four hundred and thirty years earlier. Lack of freedom had marked their experience for several generations. And now, three days' journey into the desert, the freed slaves experienced a lack of water that evaporated their trust in God and in the leadership of Moses. Their identity was firmly rooted in being "have nots."

The One who created us had something else to say about who they were, but their souls were not attuned to hear what He had to say. Author Henri Nouwen said, "Being the Beloved expresses the core truth of our existence."[5] It had been generations since they'd lived this truth.

God provided for the children of Israel that third day, transforming the bitter water at Marah into sweet refreshment. During the following months in the School of the Desert, God invited them into their identity as His beloved children. They experienced the supernatural as He led them out of Egypt, guided them by cloud and fire of His presence, provided food and water for them, and gave them the gift of His beautiful Law.

But they weren't very receptive students. They responded to the lessons of their desert classroom by:

1. Questioning the leadership of Moses (Ex. 14:11–12)
2. Complaining about undrinkable water (Ex. 15:24)
3. Accusing Moses of trying to starve them to death (Ex. 16:3)
4. Attempting to hoard perishable manna (Ex. 16:20)
5. Ignoring Moses's command not to search for manna on the Sabbath (Ex. 16:27–29)
6. Whining (again) about a lack of water (Ex. 17:2–3)
7. Creating and worshiping the idol of a golden calf (Ex. 32)
8. Kvetching about their lot in life (Num. 11:1–2)
9. Grumbling about the lack of variety in their diet (Num. 11:4)
10. Refusing to enter the Promised Land because they were afraid (Num. 14:1–4)

They flailed and thrashed as though they were drowning in the desert, clutching their old identity as exiles as if it were a lead life preserver. The bad old days in Egypt took on a shiny new luster in their souls: Maybe it wasn't so terrible there. At least they knew what they could expect from their slave masters. And the food in Egypt had a little more variety than the relentless uniformity of manna, manna, and more manna.

Their exile hearts were on full display when they stood at the doorstep of the Promised Land a little more than a year after leaving Egypt. God led the exiles as far as they could go, but needed them to embrace their identity as pilgrims so they could follow Him the rest of the way home. They'd balked big time—ten big times, in fact, as listed above, a number with great resonance to the number of plagues God had visited upon the Egyptians. He sent His people on a remedial journey away from Canaan that would end up lasting four decades:

> Nevertheless, as surely as I live and as surely as the glory of the Lord fills the whole earth, not one of those who saw my glory and the signs I performed in Egypt and in the wilderness but who disobeyed me and tested me ten times—not one of them will ever see the land I promised on oath to their ancestors. No one who has treated me with contempt will ever see it. (Num. 14:21–23)

In the face of their fear-filled refusal to obey Him, He told His cherished ones they'd live out their identity as exiles in a remedial class in the School of the Desert for the next forty years. They'd serve as God's teaching assistants, telling the story of God's promises to their children and cultivating in those children love of the Lawgiver. And every day of those forty years, they lived with the knowledge that they'd die one by one in their desert classroom. When the last of them were gone, their pilgrim children would be free to cross the Jordan and head toward home (Deut. 6:10–11).

POOR PITIFUL ME

From our vantage point more than three thousand years later, it is easy to look at the account and say, "What was wrong with them? The children of Israel had seen miracle after miracle! God delivered them from slavery! He'd provided for them in the desert every single day! *Why didn't they get it?*"

Yes, they had the visible presence of God with them 24/7, and repeatedly experienced the way He usurped the natural order of things to show them His glory. From the first plague to the journey through the desert to the edge of the Promised Land, the School of the Desert unmasked who they were, identified every area of impoverishment in their souls, and revealed what they really believed about God.

Their enslavement had stolen so much from them including their homeland, the freedom to worship the God of their fathers, their culture, and their dignity. Sadly, what they lacked became who they were. Deeply entrenched self-pity kept them in a far more permanent prison than slavery had ever been. The desert was meant to transform them into pilgrims, but self-pity kept them in exile.

While self-pity and depression have plenty of overlap, I recognize in the Hebrew people's responses to God a deep sense of victimhood that can be summed up in two words: "Why me?" Depression tends to express itself in thoughts like, "This must be my fault," "It's not worth going on any more," or "Nothing will ever change." Self-pity lays the blame at the feet of others: "Moses, did you lead us out here only to let us die?" or "I have to take care of myself by hoarding food in the desert even though God said not to do so, since He really can't be trusted."

Literature offers us several excellent examples of characters motivated by self-pity. In *Gone with the Wind*, willful Southern belle Scarlett O'Hara is determined to extract what she wants out of life, no matter what the cost to others around her. Gollum becomes a grasping, sneaky shadow of his former self when deprived of access to power in The Lord of the Rings trilogy. Uriah Heep was a manipulative sycophant in Charles Dickens's classic novel, *David Copperfield*, motivated by a deep sense of neediness and victimhood.

When the world seems out of control and an individual (or entire community, as in the case of the Hebrew people) chooses the role of the helpless victim, they are no longer responsible for what they say or do. The word "pity," in its original usage, is rooted in piety and results in compassion and empathy for others. But when we direct that pity at ourselves, it turns something kind into something rancid. Self-pity turns our story into a tragedy with no hope of redemption. It robs us of our belovedness. It makes exiles out of us.

As summer turned to autumn in the months after our sudden uprooting and relocation, self-pity was becoming a comfortable daily habit for me. Providentially, I had the opportunity to spend time with an older person I'd known for a couple of decades. When I first met Marion, she was a frank, dry-witted office manager in her mid-fifties. A later-in-life divorce and the export of her job overseas left her unemployed at sixty. A couple of health scares and a falling out with one of her children further isolated and impoverished her. Twenty years into our friendship, I prepped for a visit with her by bracing for her well-rehearsed litany of bitter complaints about her life. "They did it to me" was the chorus.

She launched into a two decades' old story about her ex that sounded in her retelling as though it had just happened last week. I'd heard the story dozens of times before. I sipped luke-warm coffee as I acted as though I was listening to her tell me again how he'd done her wrong. I wasn't listening. I was enduring it, probably making a mental grocery list as I nodded and *tsk'd* sympathetically. Suddenly, a still small Voice interrupted me: *Listen to her.*

I was tired. So tired. I'd been listening to her for years. She was the song that never ends.

Listen to her.

I paid attention afresh to a story I'd heard dozens of times before: ". . . and he cheaped out on paying Kevin's final tuition payment because he and his new girlfriend wanted to take a cruise. A cruise! Meanwhile, what could I do except take out a loan so the kid could graduate? Then when I lost my job, I ended up on the brink of bankruptcy, all because of him. Well, him and that lousy girlfriend of his. They did it to me."

There it was: *They did it to me.* I'd been framing the story of the church and our sudden move in those exact terms. Ouch. "They" had done "it" to us, forcing us into a bewildering transition zone full of blank pages. Though I didn't want to go back, I didn't know how to move forward, either.

My self-pity served as a buffer toward the sort of reflection that would allow me to both recognize and own my failings in that past drama. My frustration with a few people abusing their power had distracted me from wholehearted service to the whole con-gregation. I'd spent too much time ruminating about the prob-lems until, by the end, the problems were all I could see. Could this experience have gone differently? Self-pity left me stewing over the "if onlys" of the past with all the sour wisdom of 20/20 hindsight. Despite the unfair actions of some people toward me, I did not have to be a victim. I needed to release the hurt to God, and with His help, begin the process of forgiving them.

As I listened to Marion continue her well-rehearsed tale of all the ways she'd been wronged, something shifted ever so slightly in me, cracking the self-protective tabernacle I'd erected around myself. Keeping God at arm's length kept me in exile. The realization was not accompanied with a movie orchestra, strings swelling in a crescendo, signaling that I was about to discover that the rest of the pages in my empty book would be filled with a guaranteed happy ending. There was just Marion sitting there, still telling her story, drinking her lukewarm coffee.

TOWARD FREEDOM

If there was one takeaway for me from the account of the first stumbling steps into freedom taken by the Hebrew people, it was that one day's declaration of absolute trust in God did not automatically translate to the next day's faithfulness.

I began to wonder what it might have sounded like if the Israelites approached God in humble dependency instead of telling Moses, "God did this to us, which makes us His victims. Could you fix this already, and while you're at it, you should know we think you stink as a leader, and by the way, in case you hadn't noticed, we're dying out here on your little wild goose chase through the desert."

Trust for each new day in the desert might have sounded like "Lord, we remember all you've done for us leading up to this day.

Even when our circumstances make no sense, we choose to trust You. We confess we are afraid, and acknowledge we are weak. Please help us!"

The eerie terrain of the Sinai desert is an inhospitable place. It strips the questions of life down to the essentials of survival including food, clothing, shelter, and safety. It was an extreme version of an existence far from the garden of Eden.

Author Marlena Graves said, "The desert heightens our senses; paradoxically, we're acutely aware of both God's presence and his seeming absence. Truths once obscure, or mentally assented to yet not experienced, suddenly stand out in sharp relief, while the superfluous recedes into the background. In the desert wilderness, miracles happen, temptations lure, and judgment occurs."[6]

God built time and space into the experience of the exiled people so they could begin to practice their new identity as pilgrims. They'd left Egypt after living there for four centuries; the School of the Desert was designed to exorcise Egypt from them. Their complaining, their disobedience, and their requests to return to a land where they'd been captives is a familiar script to any of us who have ever faced a big transition. Transition carries with it the temptation to return to the familiar past, no matter how toxic it was, rather than live in the bewildering present. Indulging this temptation keeps us living as exiles instead of learning to become pilgrims. The exile status of the Chosen People would end in the desert as step by step, year by year, they learned to trust Him as pilgrims, sustaining and guiding them.

Whether the transition zone in our lives looks like a desert or a bookstore, it is the place from which our identity can shift from exile to pilgrim. We may have responded to the call to follow Jesus and started walking. But the deserts in our lives are where we begin to discover how to follow God even when—especially when—our circumstances don't make sense.

To consider

1. Reflect on a transition you've faced in your life. What was most disorienting about it? How did you respond to the uncertainty you faced? How did you know you were on the other side of it—or are you still in the midst of it?

2. When are you most tempted toward self-pity in your life?

3. Is there a situation in your life right now where you're facing great uncertainty about your future? What are you discovering about yourself as you walk through the experience? About God?

_____
_____
_____
_____
_____
_____
_____
_____
_____
_____
_____

To pray

Oh Lord, I confess I have sometimes allowed my circumstances to determine my faith in You. And when the circumstances don't make sense, I am tempted to cope with them by complaining, self-pity, or trying to figure out how to go backwards in time to a place where things did seem to make sense.

There is no going back to Egypt. There is no return to Eden. You are waiting instead to reveal Yourself to me in the School of the Desert. When I look around me at the unfamiliar, barren landscape, I am afraid. Have You brought me to this place only to abandon me here? Is this where exile leads?

No. This is not who You are. This is not where I end.

Instead, I recognize that You are asking me to rely on You for provision and guidance. Even as I confess my concerns to You, Lord, I see that You are inviting me in faith to add my voice to the chorus of those singing the words of this psalm as their song:

> Remember the wonders he has done,
>> his miracles, and the judgments he pronounced,
> you his servants, the descendants of Abraham,
>> his chosen ones, the children of Jacob.
> He is the LORD our God;
>> his judgments are in all the earth.
>
> He remembers his covenant forever,
>> the promise he made, for a thousand generations,

> the covenant he made with Abraham,
>> the oath he swore to Isaac.
> He confirmed it to Jacob as a decree,
>> to Israel as an everlasting covenant:
> "To you I will give the land of Canaan
>> as the portion you will inherit." (Ps. 105:5–11)

I remember what You have done in the past. Jesus, You promised You'd never fail or forsake me. You called me to follow. Now please teach me how. I ask this in the name of the One who was Himself tempted in the desert for forty days. Amen.

CHAPTER 5

WARNED

Jesus mapped the geography of the pilgrim's journey with these words: "Enter through the narrow gate. For wide is the gate and broad is the road that leads to destruction, and many enter through it. But small is the gate and narrow the road that leads to life, and only a few find it" (Matt. 7:13–14).

The children of Israel discovered this narrow road had plenty of twists, switchbacks, and hairpin turns as they journeyed through the desert for forty years. While they had the presence of God with them in the form of cloud by day, fire by night to guide them, He wanted them to internalize how to follow Him by heart by the time they reached the Promised Land (Ex. 13:21–22).

Living into the identity of pilgrim means we will recognize the path we're on, as that twisty, unmapped road plays a role in forming us as followers who can navigate by heart. One person who has played a key role in helping generations to understand the nature and purpose of this narrow road is John Bunyan.

When he was a young man in seventeenth-century England, John Bunyan spent his youth partying like it was 1999. He untethered himself from the morals with which he was raised: "I had but few equals, especially considering my years, which were tender, being few, both for cursing, swearing, lying, and blaspheming the holy name of God . . . I was the very ringleader of all the youth that kept me company, into all manner of vice and ungodliness."[1] He hoped the partying would silence the conviction of the Holy Spirit dogging him at every turn.

In 1649, he married for the first time. The union gentled the twenty-one-year-old John a bit. God used the books his wife brought into the marriage to shift the direction of his life. The Bible and spiritual classics he was reading and the sermons he was hearing when he accompanied his wife to a local Separatist congregation moved John from rebellion to commitment, from exile to pilgrimage. He gave himself wholeheartedly to the One who'd been pursuing him all along.

The Separatists were the seventeenth-century equivalent of the 1960s Jesus Freaks who called out for a simple, radical, revived faith. They broke away from mainstream Anglicanism, which was in John's youth the decreed faith of England, in search of a purer form of Christianity. We call a group of these Separatists who came to America in 1620 the Pilgrims—the ones we remember each November at Thanksgiving. Though we tend to cast Pilgrim history in terms of their brave escape on the *Mayflower* from the persecution they faced in England, these fiery believers were driven by a deep desire for a pure form of Christianity.

Historian Dr. Robert Tracy McKenzie noted that it was a different kind of challenge to their faith that led these Separatists to board the Mayflower after first trying to make a go of things in Holland. He explained that the parable of the sower found in Mark 4:1–20 illustrates what was behind the Pilgrims' journey to America and the motivations of all in the Separatist camp: "As the Pilgrims saw it, the principal threat that they faced in Holland was *not the scorching sun* [of persecution], but *strangling thorns*."[2] Holland's relaxed moral culture exemplified for the Separatists ". . . the worries of this life, the deceitfulness of wealth and the desires for other things" (Mark 4:19).

Not all Separatists came to America. Some, like Bunyan, stayed behind in England. Bunyan stood against moral compromise in every form, and became a lay preacher during the 1650s. After his first wife died in 1658, he married again, and continued to draw crowds with his sermons. He also drew the ire of authorities who heard subversion in his holiness-themed messages, and he landed in prison in England in 1661. Magistrates told him he could go free if he'd lay off the preaching, but he refused. Instead, he remained steadfast in prison for the next twelve years. The prison was his desert. It was the place where he was transformed from cultural exile to spiritual pilgrim.

While incarcerated, he first penned his autobiography, *Grace Abounding to the Chief of Sinners*, which offers a compelling snapshot into John's inner world—a world filled with intense battles with temptation, doubt, and his own pride. After the book's publication in 1666, he used what he'd mined from his own soul to craft his masterwork, *The Pilgrim's Progress from This World, to That Which Is to Come,* the allegory describing the believer's journey through life.

The book has stood the test of time, though modern readers will find that Separatist preacher Bunyan occasionally takes aim in the text at a few of his religious opponents including Quakers, Catholics, and Anglicans. Even so, generations of readers have been inspired and challenged by his work. For many families, this book was the second one they'd add to their library after they purchased a family Bible. *Pilgrim's Progress* has given the church the language to talk about the spiritual journey, so a brief summary of the book is in order here—along with my suggestion to read the story for yourself. (There are modern-language adaptations in print, and you can find the text of the original online as well.) Exiles and pilgrims alike will recognize themselves in the plot.

ONCE UPON A TIME

The story opens with protagonist Christian leaving his doubting wife and children behind in the City of Destruction to journey to the Celestial City. It isn't long before he finds himself mired in the Bog of Guilt: What kind of person would abandon his own family? But his longing for his true home drives him forward. There is no turning back. As he travels, he meets Worldly Wiseman, who steers him in the wrong direction, before a course correction arrives in the form of Evangelist, who directs him to the Wicket (small, narrow) Gate. He passes through that entry point into Salvation and finds his way to the Interpreter's house. He receives further instruction and continues his journey in the company of a fellow pilgrim also fleeing the City of Destruction named Faithful.

Christian meets a trio of chained men, representing foolishness, laziness, and spiritual presumption, who attempt to discourage him. He continues onward and upward, climbing the Hill of Difficulty, where he first battles religious foes Formalist and Hypocrisy before he meets and vanquishes a roaring lion. He finds his way to the Palace Beautiful, where four celestial beings, Discretion, Piety, Prudence, and Charity, clothe Christian in the Armor of God.

As he continues onward, Christian learns to apply God's Word to each challenge he faces. Christian progresses from the Palace Beautiful into the Valley of Humility, where he encounters Apollyon, a monster bent on his destruction. After he triumphs in that battle, his journey leads him downward into the Valley of the Shadow of Death.

Christian's journey brings him next to Vanity Fair, a combination circus, fashion show, and mega-mall of materialism. His companion Faithful is martyred here because he refused to join the worship of the evil lord of the city. At various points during this leg of his journey, Christian is joined by other potentially destructive traveling companions like Talkative, who excels at religious talk without action, and Mr. By-Ends, who uses religion for personal profit and success.

He escapes the trial of Vanity Fair and the loss of his friend Faithful, and is joined by a new travel companion named Hopeful. After climbing the Hill of Lucre, he meets Lot's Wife, who encourages him to look back in the direction he's already traveled. Christian also faced temptation from Vain Confidence to take a parallel wide and smooth path instead of the narrow, difficult one he's been walking. When he chooses the tempting shortcut, he is captured and imprisoned by the Giant of Despair. After a struggle, Christian uses the Key of Promise to secure the release of Hopeful and himself.

They travel onward and upward into the Delectable Mountains, where they're refreshed by shepherds, but face the temptations of Demas, promising wealth, and Apostate, who encourages them to fall away from God. Christian is trapped in the Flatterer's net, then escapes by wielding God's Word only to be bewitched into a dream-like state by Atheist.

As he again fights free of temptation, the narrow path leads him to Beulah Land, a beautiful meadow where he is refreshed before he crosses the River of Death and enters the Celestial City.

His pilgrimage is over. He's home.

Bunyan penned a sequel to *Pilgrim's Progress* detailing the journey taken by Christian's wife, Christiana, and her adult sons and their spouses. (I'm glad Bunyan didn't leave them behind in the City of Destruction!) Their destination was the same, some of the challenges and temptations they faced were similar in nature to Christian's—but their pilgrimage was unique to each one of them. Christiana's story underscores the reality that each person who longs for union with Jesus must make the pilgrim journey for themselves.

I think John Bunyan would have loved the words penned by John Newton about a hundred years later. While few of us would link the dangers, toils, and snares of pilgrimage with grace, it is God's amazing grace indeed that is at work on the road, refining us, while at the same time accompanying and guiding us onward. I hear echoes of *Pilgrim's Progress* in the beloved hymn "Amazing Grace":

> Through many dangers, toils and snares,
> I have already come;
> 'Tis grace hath brought me safe thus far,
> And grace will lead me home.

THE GRACE OF THE NARROW ROAD

Grace is a word we throw around a lot in church. It's occurred to me on occasion that the way church people sometimes use the word "grace" makes it sound like we're talking about winning an unexpected gift certificate for a spa day. The reality is God's grace is the expression of the holy beauty of His pure, jealous love. We receive it every time we recognize we could never earn it and do not deserve it. Author Paul Zahl explains:

> Grace is a love that has nothing to do with you, the beloved.
> It has everything to do with the lover ... it has nothing to do
> with my intrinsic qualities or so-called "gifts" (whatever
> they may be). It reflects a decision on the part of the giver,
> the one who loves, in relation to the receiver, the one who
> is loved, that negates any qualifications the receiver may
> personally hold.[3]

Bunyan recognized God's grace toward him in the pilgrim's journey by the way his sin was confronted, then overcome as he walked—and even when he wandered. He also underscored throughout his allegory that there was no turning back. He consistently presented the lure of a return trip back to the City of Destruction as a toxic temptation. He wanted his readers to know that pilgrimage is always a one-way trip. He wanted them to understand the difficult journey would cost them everything but bring them life forever with their Savior.

Step-by-step submission to Him is the language of grace for the pilgrim. Pastor Dietrich Bonhoeffer, who died at the hands of the Nazis during World War II, famously explained that "spa-day" grace is a cheap imitation of the real thing: "Cheap grace is grace without discipleship, grace without the cross, grace without Jesus Christ, living and incarnate."[4]

Forty years in the desert taught the Chosen People that grace wasn't cheap. It had cost them the faux comfort of Egypt, and the true comfort of the presence of their mothers and fathers, who'd died off one by one throughout four decades of wandering. They'd lived the sweetness of the Law in that desert greenhouse as they were tutored daily in the goodness and character of God. The Law was God's gift to them, and as they entered the Promised Land, God reminded them they were supposed to be His gift to the world He made and loved (Isa. 49:6).

Author Jeff Manion explains how this was to work:

Once they entered the Land of Promise, the Israelites were to live differently than the people groups in the surrounding regions; they were to live as God reflectors. The commandments—do not murder, do not steal, do not commit adultery, honor your father and mother, and so on—were to set Israel apart among the nations. The idea was that others would be drawn to the Creator God—whose character is marked by faithfulness, truth, dependability, and honor—because of their encounters with this faithful, truthful, dependable, honorable people. The Israelites were to demonstrate through their lives what the Creator God is like.

Traders traveling the caravan routes connecting Babylon with Egypt would be able to take tales of this strange people from nation to nation. I can hear them saying, "You don't have to lock your door, because theft is virtually unheard of. We could sleep at night without fear of being killed or of our cargo being plundered. There is a high level of honor and respect. They honor their parents, their neighbors, and their promises. Husbands and wives do not betray the vows they have made to each other. The hilltops are not dotted with altars to Baal or Molech. And the blessing of their God is obvious upon their lives."[5]

Before the Chosen People crossed the Jordan into the Promised Land, God gave them a final review of the lessons they'd learned in the School of the Desert. The reminder for the final was the restatement of blessings and consequences, found in Deuteronomy 28. The blessings included:

- blessing in every square inch of the land (vv. 3, 6)
- flourishing of every living thing—from children to crops (vv. 4, 8, 10)
- abundant provision and nourishment (vv. 5, 12)
- protection from enemies (v. 7)
- being rooted and established in the land (v. 9)
- serving as a beacon and leader of other nations (v. 13)

The consequences of not obeying God's Law included:

- no place of refuge or sanctuary (v. 16)
- disease, famine, and barrenness (vv. 17–24, 38–42, 48–62)
- defeat and complete disgrace among all the nations of the earth (vv. 25–29)
- oppression in every way imaginable (vv. 30–37)
- enslavement by foreigners (vv. 43–57)

The final curse in the achingly sad list of consequences for God's pilgrim people in Deuteronomy 28 is the promise of exile and dispersion (vv. 63–66). Forced exile was like a nightmarish upside-down, backwards version of the pilgrim identity. Yet even in these words, grace exists. There is, even for the rebels, ragamuffins, and spiritual refugees, a way of return. The Law prescribed how to express repentance for the Chosen People. And Jesus, the One who fulfilled every perfect stroke of the Law, came to show us the way back to the Father (John 14:6).

But as we follow Him, we learn the same lessons the Children of Israel learned as they crossed the Jordan and stepped into the Promised Land. The road is just as narrow on the other side of the Jordan as it is in the desert.

To consider

1. Bunyan uses the literary device of personification in *Pilgrim's Progress* to describe a disciple's life, turning virtues, vices, trials, and temptations into characters in the story. As you review the summary of the book included in this chapter, which episode of Christian's life resonates most with you? Why?

2. Bonhoeffer gave us the phrase "cheap grace." What does this look like in practice?

3. In Deuteronomy 28, God spelled out a list of both blessings and curses tied to the choices made by the Chosen People as to whether they'd choose to obey God or not. How are these consequences an expression of God's grace?

To pray

Dear Jesus, Your way is a narrow-road way. And every shortcut I attempt adds miles to my journey as I seek to follow after You.

You do not call me to anything You do not fully understand. Hebrews 4:15 tells me You empathize with my human frailties. You've faced every temptation I could ever face, yet You did not sin. Throughout Your Word, You show me that obedience brings me the blessing of unimpeded relationship with You. You fight for me as I face temptation. And when I wander, You are more than willing to guide me back to the narrow path.

As I consider the ways in which I've wandered from You, I pray some of the words of the song of Your servant David, a man who knew both exile and pilgrimage in his life:

> Have mercy on me, O God, according to your unfailing love; according to your great compassion blot out my transgressions. Wash away all my iniquity and cleanse me from my sin. For I know my transgressions, and my sin is always before me. Against you, you only, have I sinned and done what is evil in your sight; so you are right in your verdict and justified when you judge. . . . Create in me a pure heart, O God, and renew a steadfast spirit within me. (Ps. 51:1–4, 10)

It is Your grace that finds me when I've wandered from You, and it is Your grace that guides me back to You.

And every bit of it is amazing grace.

Thank you, Jesus, for Your sacrifice on the cross for me. Thank you for Your resurrection, which enables me to repent, return to You, and empowers me to follow You. In Your name I pray all these things.

Amen.

CHAPTER 6

DIVIDED

When my mom was dying, one of the hospice social workers talked with her about her life's unfinished business: Were there broken relationships she hoped to mend? People she wanted to see? Anyone she wished to reconnect with one more time?

My mom prided herself on her ability to hold a grudge. She'd always believed unforgiveness was a sign of strength. She shot me a warning glance before she answered the social worker's question, then shook her head firmly. "No. There's no one."

The social worker noted my mom's attempt to silence me and turned her attention in my direction. "Can you tell me about your mom's family? Does she have any siblings?"

I met the social worker's gaze and summarized the complicated story. "My mom's biological mom died shortly after giving birth to her. Her dad couldn't care for a young baby, so a cousin living in another city stepped forward to adopt her. It was the 1930s, and the prevailing wisdom of the day was to keep the adoption secret. My mom found out the truth shortly before her wedding at age eighteen."

"Wow, that must have been a terrible shock," the social worker said.

My mom glared at me, and I reminded her as gently as I could that the old rules she'd used to live her life didn't apply now.

"She has reconnected with her biological brother in adulthood," I said, "but hasn't seen her adopted brother, Warren, since their adopted father's funeral more than twenty years ago."

The social worker turned to my mom. "Would you like us to try to track him down? Is there anything you'd like to say to him?"

My mom spit her no, and then turned to stare at the wall. The conversation was over.

My younger sister decided to do a little sleuthing, just in case our mom changed her mind. She learned that our mom's adopted brother had died two years earlier. We decided not to share the information with our mom since she'd already made it clear to us she buried her relationship with Warren long ago and had no desire to see it resuscitated. My sister and I believed something terrible had happened between the two, but we never learned what it was.

During the last weeks of my mom's life, I came to understand that her long-standing grudge against Warren might have been the foundation for the many other grudges she carried. Unforgiveness sheltered her like a bunker. Division from others promised to give her what she thought she needed most—protection from any more hurt in her life.

TORN ASUNDER

Division happens when something whole is split apart. It can be a gift; when cells divide, it is because they're growing. But when people divide, it is usually the fruit of strife or sin. In cases where a rift follows abuse, addiction, or abandonment, division can preserve and nourish the healthier, growing party in the relationship. Even so, necessary division often leads to some form of exile for one or both parties involved.

In ancient Israel, after generations of slavery, another generation of School of the Desert, and years of slowly finding their way to peace in the Promised Land, King David had made the land the home of the Chosen People. By the end of his reign, there was no more warfare. No more wandering. It was a time of incredible shalom—goodness, wholeness, and peace for all. Though David didn't do it perfectly (Exhibit A: his interactions with Uriah and Uriah's wife, Bathsheba, see 2 Sam. 11–12), the arc of his life was characterized by his desire to love and honor God (1 Sam. 13:14; Acts 13:22).

To get a snapshot of David's relationship with God, you need look no further than David's expressed desire to build a permanent house of worship for his people. God told David his own history of bloodshed in regards to Uriah disqualified him for this sacred duty, but David's heir (the second son Bathsheba bore to him, Solomon) would have the privilege of building a temple to replace the tabernacle the children of Israel had been using to meet with God since the time of their desert wanderings (1 Chron. 17).

A permanent house of worship seemed to proclaim to the entire world that the Chosen People were indeed home in the Promised Land. Yet God wanted His people—even at home in the land of Israel—to remember who they were called to be: pilgrims. He built into their rhythms of worship three festivals a year where every man, woman, and child were to leave farm and household so they could travel to Jerusalem to worship.[1]

Pilgrimage had been imprinted on the children of Abraham, Isaac, and Jacob in the desert. But so had their identity as exiles. Who were they going to be?

As Solomon's four-decade reign wore on, the peace, luxury, and wealth he inherited from his father David robbed him of the gift of single-minded commitment to his father's God. Even as he was involved in building a magnificent temple, he drifted into idolatry, mixing worship of God with the worship of the gods of his many wives (1 Kings 11:1–8). Solomon's mix-and-match approach to faith flew in the face of the first two of the Ten Commandments:

"You shall have no other gods before me.

"You shall not make for yourself an image in the form of anything in heaven above or on the earth beneath or in the waters below. You shall not bow down to them or worship them; for I, the LORD your God, am a jealous God, punishing the children for the sin of the parents to the third and fourth generation of those who hate me, but showing love to a thousand generations of those who love me and keep my commandments." (Ex. 20:3–6)

Solomon's idolatry would prove to be costly. The Lord spoke to the king, telling him this beautiful unified kingdom would be torn and divided during the reign of his heir, Rehoboam (1 Kings 11:33).

In the day-to-day life of Israel, an ambitious and capable official named Jeroboam made a name for himself as a solid leader.[2] He caught the notice of his fellow citizens and slowly developed a following during Solomon's final years. He caught the notice of God too.

A prophet named Ahijah came to see Jeroboam and told him that because the people had followed their leader Solomon into idolatry, God would use Jeroboam to lead most of the wayward people. God would preserve the region of Judah, centered in Jerusalem alone under the rule of Solomon's descendants for the sake of the covenant promise He'd made to David (2 Sam. 7:12–16).

When Solomon gets word of this prophetic encounter, he seeks Jeroboam's life. Jeroboam flees the country, and Solomon passes on his scepter to his son Rehoboam. Rehoboam demonstrates a stunning level of disrespect for the people he is about to rule by bragging about how much tougher he is than his father and tells them he's going to multiply their workload just to show them who's boss. It is as though he ignored the experience his people had while slaves in Egypt a few generations earlier. Rehoboam creates exile conditions in the middle of the Promised Land for the Chosen People.

At Rehoboam's coronation, Jeroboam returns. The story in 1 Kings 11–12 reads like the script of a bad soap opera. Trusted leader Jeroboam comes off as the kinder, gentler alternative to David's grandson Rehoboam. The people "vote" against Rehoboam, pledging their allegiance to Jereboam. As a result, civil war breaks out in Israel, and Rehoboam receives a prophetic warning to stand down. Only the region containing Jerusalem and controlled by the tribe of Judah remained under Rehoboam's control.

The first thing King Jeroboam did was give his people some idols—in an attempt to keep them from making their three-times-a-year pilgrimage to Rehoboam's Jerusalem. Specifically, he presented Israel with a pair of golden calves (1 Kings 12:25–33). Philosopher George Santayana is credited with saying, "Those who do not remember history are doomed to repeat it." I'm not sure Jeroboam forgot the history of his people, but he was determined to rewrite it so it would include idols.

They wandered into spiritual exile as they streamed to the towns of Bethel and Dan to present their offerings and gather in "worship" around the silent statues erected by Jeroboam.

OUR LI'L IDOLS

We picture the idols of the Ancient Near East as grotesque figures, distorted versions of something in creation: a many-breasted female figure, an angry animal-man, a pair of golden calves. Pastor Tim Keller writes, "The biblical concept of idolatry is an extremely sophisticated idea, integrating intellectual, psychological, social, cultural, and spiritual categories. . . . The old pagans were not fanciful when they depicted virtually everything as a god. They had sex gods, work gods, war gods, money gods, nation gods—for the simple fact that anything can be a god that rules and serves as a deity in the heart of a person or in the life of a people."[3]

We moderns tend to be proud of the fact we've "evolved" past pagan forms of worship, but our lives are packed to the rafters with things competing for the place that belongs to God alone. Idolatry took root in our DNA from the very beginning, at the fall. In the garden of Eden, when the serpent hissed "Did God really say . . . ?", the first humans used God's gift of choice to entertain their own answers to the question rather than remaining in unbroken relationship with their Creator (Gen. 3:1). That decision positioned all of humanity to gravitate toward worshiping gods of our own making.

In our culture, it is easy to point to the big three—money, sex, and power—as idols. Some may recognize the control these things have over their lives. But I'd like to suggest that most of us have a personalized collection of housebroken idols vying for our love every single day. They may be destructive little gods, like unforgiveness or addiction. They may be good gifts—like affirmation, appearance, ministry, or a relationship—that have become toxic because we've given them the power to define our worth and receive our worship. If we are afraid of who we will be without them, those things have become a golden calf.

One pervasive and oh-so-familiar idol in Christian subculture is the nuclear family. (In case you doubt this, ask a Christian single to talk with you about their experience in the church.

Most have some pretty sad tales to tell.) Former pastor Dan Bouchelle shared his observations about the focus on family in most evangelical congregations:

> A good friend of mine, who has a Ph.D. in marriage and family therapy, commented a few years ago that we have a near family cult in church. There is a vast supply of family material through Christian bookstores, radio, and TV. There are countless family seminars.... Some churches build their whole visions around strengthening family. "Traditional family values" is now synonymous with the gospel for many. It is almost as if the primary purpose of the church is to serve family.[4]

Jesus confronted the temptation to idolize family with words like "If anyone comes to me and does not hate father and mother, wife and children, brothers and sisters—yes, even their own life—such a person cannot be my disciple. And whoever does not carry their cross and follow me cannot be my disciple" (Luke 14:26–27).[5] Jesus is not saying we are to loathe our families. The Greek word *miseo* used in this verse for "hate" can mean emotional loathing, but is also used to denote preference and priority.[6] Jesus is telling us that if we live the first commandment, we will be free to respond rightly to the fifth commandment—the one about honoring our parents found in Exodus 20:12. His words direct us onto the pilgrim road, carrying our cross instead of worshiping at the altar of a faux god.

The cross—the instrument of torture, suffering, and death—is what unbundles our love from the false gods and sets us free to live a life that looks like the beautiful life of Jesus. We are free to serve. We are free to forgive. We are free to worship the Father. We are free to follow.

Idolatry wraps chains around our souls. In ancient Israel, the unified family of the children of Abraham was torn in two by the hard-heartedness of Rehoboam and the ambitions of Jeroboam. At the end of the civil strife, the regions of Judah and Benjamin remained under the leadership of David's grandson Rehoboam. The remaining ten tribal regions were known collectively as Israel, and were ruled for more than two centuries by nineteen idolatrous, spiritually compromised kings that followed in Jeroboam's footsteps.

During this dark period, the people of Israel could no longer travel into Jerusalem in Judah to worship as a single family. The idolatry of their leaders had led hundreds of thousands of people into exile. In His love, the covenant-making one true God pursued His lost sheep, sending a series of prophets including Elijah, Elisha, Amos, and Hosea to call the people to repent of their idolatry and return to Him. God's people were called to be light to these nations, but the northern tribes had succeeded only in hiding their light under a bushel for generations, until the light among them had gone out.

Proclamations like this one were typical of the message each prophet gave to the closed-hearted people of Israel:

Return, Israel, to the LORD your God.
    Your sins have been your downfall!
Take words with you
    and return to the LORD.

Say to him:

"Forgive all our sins
and receive us graciously,
　　that we may offer the fruit of our lips.
Assyria cannot save us;
　　we will not mount warhorses.
We will never again say 'Our gods'
　　to what our own hands have made,
　　　for in you the fatherless find compassion." (Hos. 14:1–3)

It was a message that fell on deaf ears. In 731 BC, the Assyrians decimated Jeroboam's Israel, carrying the best of the people into slavery and dispersing the rest among their vast empire. The people of Israel were predisposed to assimilation because they'd been worshiping the gods of the surrounding nations and lost their unique identity within a couple of generations.

Only two tribes were left to remain in relationship with God: Judah and Benjamin. Having the temple in their midst slowed their spiritual decline, but they gave themselves over to mixing their worship of God with the idolatry of their nation-neighbors. This compromise put them on the same trajectory as their cousins who'd once lived to the north. As He had with Israel, God sent a stream of prophets to Judah to call them to repentance: Joel, Isaiah, Micah, Zephaniah, Jeremiah, Habakkuk, Ezekiel, Obadiah, Haggai, Zechariah, and Malachi. The people ignored them.

In 587 BC, the Babylonians conquered the people of Judah, and marched all but the weak and infirm hundreds of miles across desert and mountains into captivity. The people of Judah had lost everything. They were now exiles.

But Babylon was not the end of the story for them. In this land of exile, they discovered what it meant to own the identity of pilgrim for themselves.

To consider

1. Have you experienced division in your family, your church, or in another relationship? What has the effect of this division been in your life? Is restoration possible in this situation?

2. Pastor Tim Keller noted that an idol is anything that "rules and serves as a deity in the heart of a person or in the life of a people." In our culture, those idols can be destructive things, like fame, or they can come in far more innocuous forms, like family. As you read this chapter's discussion about idolatry, are there things in your life that may have taken on too much importance in your life, becoming idols? Ask for God's help to break their hold on your heart.

3. What tempts you to compromise your spiritual convictions? In what areas are you most vulnerable?

_____

_____

_____

_____

_____

_____

_____

To pray

Heavenly Father, at once You call me to stay in relationship with my neighbors, while at the same time not compromising my relationship with You by adopting the practices or beliefs of my neighbors who do not seek You. It seems impossible to do both simultaneously.

But You say nothing is impossible with You. Please show me how to walk this narrow path with You. Keep me from the captivity of sin.

The words of Psalm 106:35–45 describe the condition of Your Chosen People, and they describe our world today:

> they mingled with the nations
> and adopted their customs.
> They worshiped their idols,
> which became a snare to them.
> They sacrificed their sons
> and their daughters to false gods.
> They shed innocent blood,
> the blood of their sons and daughters,
> whom they sacrificed to the idols of Canaan,
> and the land was desecrated by their blood.
> They defiled themselves by what they did;
> by their deeds they prostituted themselves.
>
> Therefore the LORD was angry with his people
> and abhorred his inheritance.
> He gave them into the hands of the nations,
> and their foes ruled over them.

Their enemies oppressed them
    and subjected them to their power.
Many times he delivered them,
    but they were bent on rebellion
    and they wasted away in their sin.
Yet he took note of their distress
    when he heard their cry;
for their sake he remembered his covenant
    and out of his great love he relented.

Sovereign Lord, I ask for Your help in identifying which gifts and desires have taken Your rightful place in my life. Some of my idols are obvious ones. Others, slyer. But You see each one of them clearly, and You tell me, "You shall have no other gods before me."

Holy One, there is no other God but You. I worship You. Amen.

CHAPTER 7

REMEMBERED

When you ache for a fresh start, remembering your past is the last thing you want to do.

I recently viewed a sobering documentary that illustrated this reality. It was titled *From Baghdad to Brooklyn*. The film traced the story of Mohamed, a twenty-something Iraqi man displaced to Syria by the war in his home country. His sexual orientation, his flamboyant dress, unfiltered language, and love of all things American rendered him a target in Iraq. As a refugee in Syria, he is not permitted to work, so he spends his days watching videos and aimlessly wandering the streets. To cope, he creates a story about his former life, telling new friends he was a famous model back in Iraq.

Jennifer, a well-meaning young American female journalist, was one of his new friends. She documents on film her relationship with Mohamed, showing how she worked for many months to secure asylum for him in the US. Their close but tempestuous friendship disintegrates after he arrives here, and she slowly realizes the truth about Mohamed was in plain sight the whole time. He'd never been a model. He was an emotionally fragile man who did all he could to put Iraq in the past by creating a fantasy life for himself using the tools of Western-style fame. She sadly confesses that her nurturing instincts kicked into overdrive as she ignored the signals that Mohamed was not all that he seemed. Instead, she put on blinders and made him her personal project. The relationship comes to a painful end.

As the film concludes, another filmmaker interviews Mohamed, who has cut all ties with Jennifer. He is now a hairdresser in Brooklyn and seems to recognize that the emotional and spiritual baggage he brought with him to Syria when he fled war-torn Iraq as a refugee has followed him all the way to exile in Brooklyn. Five thousand, seven hundred miles from home, he begins to unpack that baggage. As the movie concludes, he realizes sadly he is the same person he's always been. I pray he continues the process of healing.

Christians love the promise of a clean slate and a fresh start. We honor testimonies of those who once were lost, but have been found by Jesus. The more messed-up a person was "Before Christ"—especially if they were famous or notorious—the more we relish their salvation story. There is biblical precedent for this, certainly. The apostle Paul, who possessed a messed-up, murderous past, referenced his "BC" days throughout his ministry (Acts 22:2–16; Acts 26; 1 Tim. 1:16).

However, being found doesn't mean He erases our histories.

Instead, Jesus speaks of supernaturally transforming them. When the adult Nicodemus questioned Jesus about His ministry in John 3:1–20, Jesus told Nicodemus that he needed to be born again. Jesus emphasized this wasn't about getting a physical do-over, but instead about being regenerated at this point in his life by a supernatural work of the Spirit. Jesus ends His conversation to the religious leader with these words: "Everyone who does evil hates the light, and will not come into the light for fear that their deeds will be exposed. But whoever lives by the truth comes into the light, so that it may be seen plainly that what they have done has been done in the sight of God" (vv. 20–21). Even as Jesus proclaims new life, He uses language that speaks of 20/20 memory.

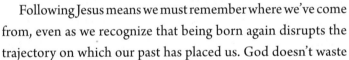

Following Jesus means we must remember where we've come from, even as we recognize that being born again disrupts the trajectory on which our past has placed us. God doesn't waste a single component of our experiences by asking us to forget. Remembering can be a holy activity.

Holy remembering isn't a navel-gazing retrospective look at our own experiences, though it includes reflection about who we are/where we've been, assessment of our strengths and weaknesses, and acknowledgment of the gifts we've been given by God by which we serve others. We can't fully know ourselves, so it is a given we will not remember any of these things with full clarity.

The kind of remembering to which God calls us has to do with our relationship with Him. The Hebrew word for "remember" is *zakar*, which captures the way in which God is bound to His covenant people: He remembers the fullness of this relationship every millisecond of eternity. Because He remembers, He acts on behalf of His people for their good in everything He does, whether it is in blessing or in discipline. His love is expressed in this kind of remembering. And He calls His people again and again to *zakar* Him. As they continually remember Him in the context of their covenant relationship, they become more fully the people He created them to be.[1]

FORGETTING TO REMEMBER

Exiles may try to manage the ache for the past via ultimately unhelpful coping mechanisms. We legislate, creating strict rules for ourselves and others so we can bring order to the chaos we're feeling. Or we seek to assimilate, trying to blend in to the surrounding culture. Others among us choose to don a pair of rose-colored glasses through which we view the past, substituting nostalgia for true *zakar*.

The Bible's account of what happened after the kingdom of Israel split into ten northern tribes collectively called Israel and two southern tribes, which were known as Judah, is a story of forgetting—and then, the healthy recovery of memory. In the previous chapter, we traced the story of Israel's downfall. After they were conquered and carried away by the Assyrians in 722 BC, the only people still in relationship with God were the people of Judah.

Seeing their northern cousins vanquished and uprooted didn't jolt the people of Judah into holy remembering. Instead, they treated their adherence to temple-based worship as a magic amulet of sorts. Their thinking seemed to go along the lines of "As long as we do our God stuff, what would it matter if we also dabbled a bit with the idols of our neighbor-nations?" They engaged in the same sort of mix-and-match syncretism as Israel had, combining one part worship prescribed by the Torah with an equal part of idol worship: "Even while these people were worshiping the LORD, they were serving their idols" (2 Kings 17:41).

Though most of Judah's kings were more than happy to lead people in mix-and-match religion, there were a few rulers who were willing to remember the one true God. Second Kings 22 tells the story of the best of the lot, Josiah. He became king at age eight, in 632 BC. Despite the fact that his own father was a lousy role model, Josiah was a straight arrow, aimed at the heart of God (2 Kings 22:2).

At age eighteen, Josiah orders some repairs made to the temple, and the workmen discover the long-neglected Torah scrolls. As Josiah reads through them, a slow horror rises in him. Among the other ways they'd failed their God, he realizes recent generations of his royal forebears had never taken the time to inscribe their own personal copy of the scrolls in the presence of the priests, a command given in Deuteronomy 17:18. As the king did this, he would learn every syllable of it for himself. Josiah threw himself into obedience, and he rightly remembered God and His good commands, as well as who His people were meant to be. He calls them to repentance and leads them back to God.

Sadly, this didn't last long. When Josiah's oldest son became king, he reverted to idol worship (2 Kings 23:31–35). After his short reign, Josiah's second son took the throne and continued what his brother had started. Two more kings followed this same self-destructive path. As a result, Judah grew weaker and weaker, both spiritually and militarily.

By 589 BC, the Babylonians had been at war with Judah for several years and laid siege to Jerusalem. The battle lasted perhaps eighteen months. The book of Lamentations describes in vivid language what this siege was like for those living within the walls of the holy city. Here's a sample:

> But now they are blacker than soot;
>> they are not recognized in the streets.
> Their skin has shriveled on their bones;
>> it has become as dry as a stick.
>
> Those killed by the sword are better off
>> than those who die of famine;
> racked with hunger, they waste away
>> for lack of food from the field.
>
> With their own hands compassionate women
>> have cooked their own children,
> who became their food
>> when my people were destroyed. (Lam. 4:8–10)

The Babylonians broke through in 586/7 BC, looting and destroying the temple and the city surrounding it. The best and strongest of the people were marched nine hundred miles from Judah and turned into worker bees in Babylonian society. The old, sick, and weak were left behind to fend for themselves in the devastated land. If they were following the script for all other vanquished peoples in the ancient Near East (including Israel), this would have been the end of them. They would be a people no more.

But far from home, the people of Judah remembered. Author Jen Pollock Michel notes, "If the Bible testifies to the joy of home, the bulk of the narrative witnesses to the grief of its loss."[2] Nowhere is this grief more obvious than in the material connected to the Babylonian exile.

Listen to the ache and anguish of remembering found in Psalm 137:

> By the rivers of Babylon we sat and wept
>> when we remembered Zion.
> There on the poplars
>> we hung our harps,
> for there our captors asked us for songs,
>> our tormentors demanded songs of joy;
>> they said, "Sing us one of the songs of Zion!"
>
> How can we sing the songs of the LORD
>> while in a foreign land?
> If I forget you, Jerusalem,
>> may my right hand forget its skill.
> May my tongue cling to the roof of my mouth
>> if I do not remember you,
> if I do not consider Jerusalem
>> my highest joy.

Remember, LORD, what the Edomites[3] did
    on the day Jerusalem fell.
"Tear it down," they cried,
    "tear it down to its foundations!"
Daughter Babylon, doomed to destruction,
    happy is the one who repays you
    according to what you have done to us.
Happy is the one who seizes your infants
    and dashes them against the rocks.

Selah. Pause for a moment, and let those words sink in. This is what *zakar*—holy remembering—can sound like.

When in Babylon, the people of Judah owned the truth: their ongoing disobedience to God was the single factor that led them there. As part of His covenant relationship with them, He'd long warned them that they would lose their land if they strayed from His commandments. In response, they repented.

Jewish leaders sought to shepherd their people in Babylon, reinterpreting the parts of the Law dependent on access to the temple so the people could seek God right where they were. Most importantly, they didn't assimilate in order to blend into Babylonian society. The books of Daniel and Esther both recorded events that took place during the Babylonian captivity. They demonstrate some of the ways the Chosen People maintained their remembered identity.

Remembering also carried a deeply emotional component for the people. Psalm 137 demonstrates the ache for home—an ache that resided in the very marrow of their bones. This keen ache is bound up in memory.

TOWARD HOME

Jesus illustrates the navigational power of the ache of being up-rooted in what surely must be His most beloved parable—the story of the prodigal son found in Luke 15:11–32. We honor the insight embedded in the father's interaction with his legalistic older son in the second half of the story, but most of us especially love the first half of the parable featuring the self-imposed exile from his family by the younger son. The young man demands his inheritance, partying like a rock star and burning through the money in short order. He hits bottom during a time of famine. He takes a job feeding (non-kosher!) pigs. And then he remembered.

> "When he came to his senses, he said, 'How many of my
> father's hired servants have food to spare, and here I am starv-
> ing to death! I will set out and go back to my father and say to
> him: Father, I have sinned against heaven and against you. I
> am no longer worthy to be called your son; make me like one
> of your hired servants.'" (Luke 15:17–19)

The words "he came to his senses" mean, literally, "he came to himself." The younger son snapped out of his wrong thinking about God, the world, and himself. He woke up, recovering his true identity as a result. He was beloved son of a gracious, gen-erous father. The truth set him free to repent, to turn in a new direction, and to take the first steps toward home. No longer an exile, he'd begun his pilgrim journey.

When the prodigal people in Babylon were willing to do some holy remembering, they finally saw clearly through their tears of repentance, too. Judah was not a place of spiritual oppression where their controlling God was prohibiting them from doing as they pleased. Instead, it was a land of peace, flowing with milk and honey and filled with the presence of a Father waiting to welcome them home.

God had set a timer on their lives in Babylon though it must have seemed an impossible dream in the day-to-day existence of the exiles. After seventy years, the conquered people would be permitted to return to Judah.[4] God moved on the heart of a Persian king, Cyrus, who'd come to power in Babylon and permitted some Jews living in Babylon to return to a home it is likely few of them had ever seen—but they'd all learned to remember.

Though a portion of the Jewish community settled in Babylon (modern-day Iraq) for the next two thousand years through the end of World War II, their story is not the one highlighted in Scripture. The pilgrim journey homeward, described in vivid detail by Ezra and Nehemiah, is the one we wanderers are called to remember.

To consider

1. Have you ever attempted to start over in your life, perhaps by moving to a new city? If so, do you feel it gave you the fresh beginning for which you'd hoped? What parts of your former life carried into your new life?

2. What parts of your history do you wish you could forget? Why?

3. How can holy remembering help you better understand your past? How can it shift the way you understand your present?

_____

_____

_____

_____

_____

_____

_____

_____

_____

_____

_____

_____

_____

_____

_____

_____

_____

To pray

Merciful God, I've experienced division in my family, in my church, in my community, and in my country. Please reveal to me the places where I've contributed to it, and guide me as to how I am to act as Your agent of reconciliation where I can.

Even as I pray these words, I confess I am overwhelmed. No matter where I wander or on which side of the dividing line I find myself, my truest longing is for a place I've never been. This I know: I am far from home.

David's song is my prayer: "You, God, are my God, earnestly I seek you; I thirst for you, my whole being longs for you, in a dry and parched land where there is no water" (Ps. 63:1). May my sacred remembering become the kind of longing that transforms my exile into the sure and stumbling steps of my pilgrim journey.

I pray these words in the name of the One who came to show us the way home.

Amen.

CHAPTER 8

TREKKED

Secular pilgrimage" is a growing trend. I've known some intrepid seekers who've made their way to Inca citadel Machu Pichu in Peru, the Angkor Wat temple complex in Cambodia, or hiked the Appalachian Trail. Secular pilgrimages may include some of the usual things that go along with standard tourist experiences: sightseeing, searching for souvenirs, and discovering the right backdrops for the perfect selfie. But the primary focus of secular pilgrimage is discovering spiritual connection with oneself, nature, and/or history.

The British Pilgrimage Trust, an organization designed to highlight England's historic sacred routes and sites, tells visitors on its website, "British pilgrimage is open to all, with or without religion. Bring your own beliefs."[1]

A generation ago, author Eugene Peterson offered an insight as to the motivation driving the growth of this trend: "There is a great market for religious experience in our world; there is little enthusiasm for the patient acquisition of virtue, little inclination to sign up for a long apprenticeship in what earlier generations of Christians called holiness."[2]

British Catholic writer Dan Hitchens noted that secular pilgrimage is "a very 21st-century kind of spirituality."[3] Hitchens challenges the notion of these spiritual-but-secular experiences designed to help seekers commune with nature or discover themselves by asking if these trips are truly pilgrimages in the classic sense of the word:

> It's a complex question, but as far as Christianity goes I think the answer is probably no. Jesus provoked not so much "a sense of wonder" as fear, astonishment, fiercely personal hatred and even more fiercely personal love. He spoke about individual fulfilment, but said that the only way to it was a slow death by crucifixion. He showed compassion, but often in startling ways—negotiating with devils, controlling the weather, raising the dead. It was not your average Ted talk.[4]

We who seek to follow Jesus frame discipleship through the lens of pilgrimage. Does this mean that taking an actual physical journey to a place of pilgrimage has no place in our lives?

On the contrary. Though not in any way mandatory, many have found that dedicating time and resources toward making a pilgrimage journey can catalyze their desire for transformation. Phileena Heuertz, who, along with her husband, walked more than five hundred miles of the Camino de Santiago (Way of St. James) pilgrimage route through Spain to the traditional burial spot of the apostle, explained, "Whether we are walking to a holy site or being mindful of our spiritual life, in both cases we can willfully embark on the journey or not. The choice is ours: either we decide to journey in hope of growth and change or we resign to life as it is."[5]

Many of us think of prayer as something we do with heart and mind. We don't always consider what it means to pray with our bodies, but discipleship always involves our physical selves as well as our inner lives. A physical pilgrimage can reconnect our body to our soul. An acquaintance of mine, Fran, walked the Camino pilgrim route during thirty-six days in the summer of 2016. She told me, "The prayer of the body that a pilgrimage, any pilgrimage, offers is a real gift. Whether you are walking around the block or on the Way of St. James, it is a chance to truly be transformed." A year after she completed the Camino journey, she reports that her life has changed in ways both deep and permanent: "The pilgrimage changed everything for me. I find that I am called to a simpler life and that I worry less."

Some Christians making modern pilgrimages to sacred sites are seeking a place of encounter with God. In this desire to experience connection with the divine beyond themselves, they may share a distant kinship with some of those making secular pilgrimages. However, for the Christian, the experience of traveling in a sacrificial manner to a holy destination can serve to strengthen their faith and illumine the contours of the narrow road they're already walking. The ancient Celts called locations where the divine seemed especially near "thin places." Though God is present everywhere at all times, Scripture tells us there are specific sites God designated to meet with His people: with

Moses at the burning bush in the desert, at Mt. Sinai as He gave Moses the Law, and most notably, at the tabernacle—particularly in the Holy of Holies—and then, after Israel inhabited the Promised Land, at the temple in Jerusalem.

While modern notions of thin places lean heavily toward places thick with the invitation to introspection and spiritual renewal, pastor Mark Roberts noted that in the Old Testament, the temple—the ultimate thin place—was anything but quiet: "The Temple was not . . . a place of worship like a synagogue or church sanctuary. Nor was it a quiet place for retreat, at least not in the courts where ordinary folk were welcome. The Temple, by its very design, kept people away from its holiest places, the places where God was said to dwell and where priests alone could enter. Yet common people surely experienced God's presence in the Temple courts, and in this sense those courts constituted a thin place."[6]

Under the new covenant, our bodies—our very selves—are the temple. His Spirit resides within us and with us. We aren't bound by law to make thrice-yearly pilgrimages to a specific place to worship. But the act of pilgrimage to a holy place can be a transformative experience for those who feel led to make such a journey.

I have been to Jerusalem seven times. It is the ultimate pilgrimage destination for the believer, filled with Bible history at every turn, and the opportunity to walk where Jesus walked. Of course, Christians don't have a corner on Jerusalem. Jews and Muslims lay claim to the city, too, and it serves as flashpoint of ages-old political tensions between the three faiths. In some ways, it is like any other urban area, full of the daily bedlam of people conducting business, raising families, and talking into their cellphones. (So many cellphones!) Every historic spot in the Old City is filled with tourists taking pictures to prove they were there. Yet, it is undeniable there is still an imprint of the presence of God in the place, mixed with the longing of the devout and the spiritual hunger of the curious who make the journey to the Holy City. Despite the long history of religious and political tensions, and the daily cacophony of modern life, many pilgrims continue to report thin place experiences there, sometimes when they're least expecting it.

The first time my husband and I arrived in Jerusalem, we'd flown through the night and had been awake more than twenty-four hours. When we arrived at our hotel, it was too early to check into our room, so we stowed our bags with the hotel clerk, ate something, and decided we'd go for a walk. We set out in the general direction of the Old City, but quickly realized the little plastic tourist map I was carrying would be of no use once we entered the Jaffa Gate. Those narrow, crowded ancient streets and twisting, shadowed alleyways were a baffling maze to both of us, particularly in our sleep-deprived state.

We had no specific destination in mind. Like many married couples, when Bill and I are lost, we tend to bicker a bit. Not that day. It was as though an unseen hand was guiding us to exactly where we needed to go. We just kept walking, not stopping to look or shop or take pictures. A turn, then another and another, down a steep hill as we dodged cabs and wove our way through crowds—and there it was: the Western Wall.

This span of ancient Jerusalem stone is an intact piece of the temple's presence on this spot until the holy place was destroyed by the Romans in AD 70. The Western Wall is a place of deep longing, collective sorrow, and the locus of generations of imprecations and praise from pilgrims. It is the physical link to the beauty of a temple once filled with the presence of God and the longing among the Jewish people for a Messiah to reign on the earth in perfect justice and pure mercy.

Bill and I weren't trying to find the wall. We had plans to visit a couple of days later. Our agenda didn't matter. When we stood in front of that holy and heartbreaking wall, the realization that we'd been drawn there like exhausted moths to a flame was life-altering for me. In that moment and place, my own ache for home—an ache that has marked the diaspora experience of my people—was simultaneously exposed and salved, my identity as a Jewish follower of Jesus was affirmed within me in a place too deep for words. My trust grew in the Holy Spirit's faithfulness in leading us exactly where we need to go, every step of our journey.

We were standing in a thin place.

Many of us have had these experiences even when we haven't traveled a step. These moments during a time of worship or prayer, during a period of great sorrow or trial can undo us with an overwhelming awareness of God's nearness, holiness, and love. Eternity invades time, and the membrane between heaven and earth seems thin as silk. It takes a pilgrim to breathe the atmosphere there.

Yet thin places are not a permanent destination. Jesus' disciples found themselves in a thin place when they experienced the transfiguration of Jesus and a visitation from Moses and Elijah (Matt. 17:1–13). Peter offered to build shelters for the visitors and his friend Jesus—perhaps to capture permanently the thin place experience. They discovered that the experience had little to do with staying put. It was, at least in part, meant to illumine their understanding of who Jesus was and nurture their obedience to Him as they continued their pilgrim journey with Him.

SINGING THEIR WAY HOME

Our wanderings can't be defined by either the dabblings of those who are spiritual tourists or the drive to put down roots in a place that's not home, becoming spiritual settlers. The story of the Chosen People's return from Babylon underscores the temptations unique to the pilgrim.

Though they'd once lived in close proximity to the thin place of the temple, their years of idolatry had given them thick skins and hard hearts that numbed them to God's ways and had nearly snuffed out their ability to reflect His light to the world (Isa. 49:6). It took Babylon to show them just how far they'd wandered from God. Exile peeled away those callouses. And when the calouses were gone, the Chosen People grieved for what they'd left behind.

Back before the exile, when they were still living in Judah, God promised the people of Judah through the prophet Jeremiah there would be an end to their displacement: "This is what the LORD says: 'When seventy years are completed for Babylon, I will come to you and fulfill my good promise to bring you back to this place'" (Jer. 29:10; also Jer. 25). This promise must have seemed as impossible to the exiles as the one made to their forebears that they'd be set free from hundreds of years of slavery in Egypt (Gen. 15:13–14).

In the Ancient Near East, once a people were conquered, they were absorbed into the victor's culture. It was the end of them as a nation. But exile in Babylon transformed the people of Judah into pilgrim people. Babylon was, in the words of the famous quote from Star Trek, a real-life "assimilate or die" experience for the Jewish people. The Jewish community embraced their status as aliens and outsiders. During their first years in Babylon, Jewish scribes and teachers set to work trying to figure out how their people could reconnect with God via obedience to the Law without a temple in which to center their worship. Prayer and study of the Law grew in importance as a way in which the exiles could continue to worship God.

Babylon fell in 540 BC to the invading Persian army. Cyrus I became the ruler of the land. One of his first acts was to permit those from the community of Judean exiles to return to Jerusalem if they chose to do so (Ezra 1). This stunning declaration flew in the face of standard political and military practice, but Cyrus I noted in his proclamation that "the LORD, the God of heaven" had called him to rebuild the temple in Jerusalem.

In total, more than forty thousand people made the journey back to Judah (Ezra 2:64), most to a land they'd never seen but had heard about through the tales of their parents and grandparents and for which they'd prayed throughout their captivity. Every step of that journey homeward helped them begin to shed the identity of exile and more deeply inhabit who they were meant to be: pilgrims. As they approached Jerusalem, it's quite possible they sang the songs their Hebrew forebears had sung three times a year as they made their final climb upward into the hills of Jerusalem in order to celebrate Passover, Shavuot, and Sukkot (Deut. 16:16). These songs, found in Psalms 120–134, are known collectively as the Psalms (or Songs) of Ascent.

Author Eugene Peterson said of these psalms, "For those who chose to live no longer as tourists but pilgrims, the Songs of Ascent combine all the cheerfulness of a travel song with the practicality of guidebook and map."[7] They are the soundtrack of the disciple and are written to the cadence of one-foot-in-front-of-the-other journeying homeward.

These travel songs reflect a variety of themes familiar to any pilgrim:

PSALM 120
Plea for God's help against enemies

PSALM 121
Trust in God's protection

PSALM 122
Longing to be in Jerusalem to worship God in the temple

PSALM 123
Entreaty for God's mercy in the face of mockers

PSALM 124
Gratitude for God's assistance and care

PSALM 125
Confidence in God's justice

PSALM 126
Prayer for the promise-keeping God to set things right

PSALM 127
Affirmation of the beauty of a life built on God alone

PSALM 128
Blessing of living in obedience to God

PSALM 129
Appeal for God's justice against oppressors

PSALM 130
Hope in the God who forgives

PSALM 131
Confidence and rest in surrender to God

PSALM 132
Recollection of God's promises to David and all Israel

PSALM 133
Rejoicing in the unity of a community serving God together

PSALM 134
Celebration of the sweetness and beauty of serving God

Peterson notes the subject and audience of these songs is God: "Do you think the way to tell the story of the Christian journey is to describe its trials and tribulations? It is not. It is to name and describe God who preserves, accompanies and rules us."[8]

We Christian moderns emphasize the importance of owning and sharing our story. But the Songs of Ascent remind us that our stories are hollow echoes if they're not centered on the One who is their author.

SETTLING DOWN

The melody from the Songs of Ascent segued into the rhythm of tools on stone and wood as the pilgrims set to work rebuilding the temple. Almost immediately, they faced opposition from some of the non-Jewish people who'd taken up residence in Judah. The campaign of gossip, fear-mongering, and bribery of local officials by these opponents brought rebuilding to a halt for fourteen years (Ezra 4). The great burst of energy fueling the return to the devastated territories of Judah and Benjamin dissipated as the pilgrims sought to unpack their bags and settle down once and for all.

The business of being a settler is at odds with the life of a pilgrim. Settlers prioritize security and comfort in ways that leave them vulnerable to the temptation toward spiritual compromise with those around them. If we believe we've "arrived" somehow, there's no need to keep the compass we used on our journey. There's no need to sing pilgrim songs or long for thin places. In the case of the returnees to Judah, it seemed so much easier to seek peace with their Gentile neighbors through intermarriage, dabbling in idol worship, and leaving the repair of the rest of the ruined, neglected city for someone else to do at some unspoken point in the future.

Most returnees settled outside the city walls of Jerusalem and unplugged from the spiritual compass they'd used to direct them homeward. Though they lived near the ruined temple, they chose to inhale the polluted air of the world around them rather than the life-giving oxygen of the thin place.

It took words from God brought to the people by the

prophets Haggai and Zechariah to awaken the people once again to their mission.[9] The people finally finished rebuilding the temple about twenty years after they first started. Several decades after the people of Judah were first given permission to return, another Persian king named Artaxerxes sent the well-respected teacher of the Law, Ezra, from Babylon to Jerusalem to ensure that the Jewish people living there were honoring God. Artaxerxes appears to have taken to heart Cyrus I's deep respect for the God of the Chosen People. Artaxerxes funded Ezra's journey and invited him to gather a large group of willing exiles living in Babylon to make the long, dangerous journey with him.

Ezra describes how they prepped for the trip:

> There, by the Ahava Canal, I proclaimed a fast, so that we might humble ourselves before our God and ask him for a safe journey for us and our children, with all our possessions. I was ashamed to ask the king for soldiers and horsemen to protect us from enemies on the road, because we had told the king, "The gracious hand of our God is on everyone who looks to him, but his great anger is against all who forsake him." So we fasted and petitioned our God about this, and he answered our prayer. (Ezra 8:21–23)

The fasting and prayer oriented them to their journey. The exiles were entitled to the king's protection for their journey since he's the one who'd commissioned them to go. Instead, they elected to trust God to protect and guide them as a testimony to the king. It tuned their ears to the themes found in the Songs of Ascent as they traveled.

By the time they arrived in Jerusalem, their songs had turned to tears. Ezra was devastated to discover his people had once again been engaged in spiritual compromise with their Gentile neighbors, most notably, through intermarriage, a practice against which God had specifically warned them (Deut. 7:1–5; Ezra 9). Ezra's mourning was public, emotional, and loud. As he interceded for his people, he asked God, "Shall we then break your commands again and intermarry with the peoples who commit such detestable practices? Would you not be angry enough with us to destroy us, leaving us no remnant or survivor?" (Ezra 9:14).

He knew the answer.

Ezra believed the people needed a spiritual purgative so they could reboot their relationship to God, themselves, one another, and the nations around them. The book of Ezra ends with a census unlike any other in Scripture. It is a listing by family and names of all those who'd intermarried. In the Ancient Near East, marriage had little to do with love or romance. It was primarily a contract between two families. Ezra called the people to sever these unholy alliances so they'd be free to honor and obey the holy God who had always been faithful in husbanding them.

In this same general time frame, a Jew named Nehemiah was serving the king in Babylon. Nehemiah was undone after he learned that the people in Jerusalem had settled for living around a city still in complete disrepair—a picture of their vulnerability to compromise. The king noticed his sorrow, and Nehemiah put his own life on the line as he risked asking the king for permission to leave his position in the court and return to Jerusalem to see what he could do to remedy the situation. As in the case of Ezra, Nehemiah's deep grief becomes a catalyst for action.

When he arrived in Jerusalem, he saw the beautiful temple surrounded by unrepaired devastation dating back more than a hundred years. Despite opposition from Gentile leaders living in Judah, Nehemiah organized work and security crews to make repairs to the walls and rebuild the gates protecting the city (Neh. 3–4). In addition, he took steps to right the unjust way in which the poor in the Jewish community had been taxed (Neh. 5).

After Nehemiah finished directing the rebuilding process, Ezra read aloud the Law to the people of Judah. Here at last, we see the same anguish that had once undone both Ezra and Nehemiah, grief like a tidal wave submerging the crowd as they realized the magnitude of their sin against God (Neh. 8:9). Their repentance allowed them to inhale the life-giving oxygen of the thin place, and freed them from the gravity anchoring them to the compromise of a settler's lifestyle.

They were not spiritual tourists nor were they settlers. Their repentance reframed the way in which they understood their wanderings, and they stepped fully into their identity as pilgrims as a result. The desire to obey God became the soundtrack for their shared life as His people: "Thy statutes have been my songs in the house of my pilgrimage" (Ps. 119:54 KJV).

Tourists are searching for an experience. Settlers are looking for security. Neither desire is wrong, but if we allow experiences or security to determine our journey, we will remain wanderers.

To consider

1. If you were going to plan a pilgrimage journey to a holy, historically significant location or to a place of remarkable natural beauty, where would you go? Why do you say so?

2. Read through the Songs of Ascent (Psalms 120–134) in a single sitting. What themes/passages most resonate with you? You may find it helpful to spend some extended time meditating on and praying through those passages.

3. Reflect on your spiritual journey to this point of your life. Are there times when you've been a tourist? A settler? What pressures, temptations, or desires were you responding to at those times in your life? What would pilgrimage have looked like in those circumstances?

_____

_____

_____

_____

_____

_____

_____

_____

_____

_____

_____

_____

_____

To pray

Good and gracious Father, what shock and awe the exiles in Babylon must have felt when they received word from Cyrus that they'd be allowed to return home. I taste a bit of that kind of joy when I obey You.

As I submit my life to You, You repurpose my wanderings. You waste nothing. Instead, You make meaning of every step I take. My exile experience bears witness to Your faithfulness. There is nowhere I may wander that You are not waiting for me, calling me to return to You.

I can't find my way home to You on my own, Lord. As I seek to follow You, I pray these words will tell my story, too:

> When the LORD restored the fortunes of Zion,
>   we were like those who dreamed.
> Our mouths were filled with laughter,
>   our tongues with songs of joy.
> Then it was said among the nations,
>   "The LORD has done great things for them."
> The LORD has done great things for us,
>   and we are filled with joy.
>
> Restore our fortunes, LORD,
>   like streams in the Negev.
> Those who sow with tears
>   will reap with songs of joy.
> Those who go out weeping,
>   carrying seed to sow,

will return with songs of joy,
    carrying sheaves with them. (Ps. 126)

Streams normally don't flow in the desert. Nor do losses and grief result in joy and abundance. But I know You are the God who does impossible things.

You are the resurrection. You are life.

You call me, and I turn to You. I take a step. Then another. You have made me a pilgrim.

Amen.

CHAPTER 9

SOJOURNED

I envy some of those who've been members of a single church for their entire lives. At this point of my life, given the number of places we've lived and churches my family has attended, I recognize this will never be my experience.

There have been times when we've left a church even though we haven't relocated. We've experienced the spiritual chaos of bad leadership coupled with unrepentant sin. We've experienced the spiritual chaos caused by leaders who have stolen money from the congregation, engaged in sexual sin of every variety, abused their power, or pretzeled biblical truth into "almost-true" lies. My husband and I would prayerfully wrestle with our decision about whether it was better to stay in a dysfunctional situation in hopes of helping to bring positive change or whether it was wiser to simply move on.

In most cases, because our family tended to be newer to the congregation and didn't have the same loyalties and social ties that bound long-time members to one another, we ended up moving on. But leaving these congregations rarely felt as neat or simple as the natural transitions that accompany a graduation, job change, or relocation. Instead, they usually felt more like a divorce as relationships were severed, trust violated, and hurt filled the jagged space between estranged people and groups.

Not long ago, I was at a memorial service for a man who'd been a member of his church for fifty-five years, leaving the congregation only when he moved into a retirement community in another town. He and his wife first became members of the church when they were beginning their lives together. They raised their children in the church, and served faithfully through the decades, even as their peers gradually left the old neighborhood for warm-weather retirement communities, grew ill, or passed away. This gentleman and his wife were foundation builders, infrastructure developers, and culture creators for more than five decades in their congregation.

No doubt their church dealt with everything from shifting tastes in worship music, adapting to a variety of different pastors and leaders, and navigating the rapidly changing culture around them. Surely there were some epic intramural political battles, doctrinal skirmishes, and fights about what color the new carpet in the sanctuary should be. There must have been periods of growth and periods of decline in the congregation. What held this faithful man and his wife there all those years?

I've done an informal survey among people I know who've been long-time members of their local church. It seems those who stay for decades fall into two groups. Some stay because they value the familiar rhythms of congregational life or have a sense of owner's loyalty to their friends or even the building itself (and its carpet!). These are not bad things, but they are the choices made by settlers.

Others stay long-term because they are pilgrims. Sometimes staying put in a church is far more difficult than leaving one, especially if the congregation is going through a period of transition or division. It is possible to "pilgrim in place," blazing a trail of faithfulness through a landscape marked by disruption and confusion. And it is just as possible to be a soul in motion, pursuing God during the placid, stable times while learning to discern the difference between His peace and the settlers' temptation toward spiritual stagnation.

At some point, burned and burned out after yet another church drama, I wondered if continuing to join local churches was my act of insanity. Maybe it would be easier to quit the organized church. It's a growing trend, and the negative experiences my family and I had through the years certainly fit well with the growing demographic of those who have decided they love Jesus but have become disaffected with and disconnected from the organized church.[1]

Can you believe in Jesus and not attend church? My own story as a young believer showed me that I could. I came to faith in Jesus the Messiah when I was fifteen. My Jewish parents forbade me from attending church while I lived under their roof. They hoped my faith was a fad and attempted to starve it out.

Instead, for the next three years, I read my Bible, pirated Christian books into the house, listened to sermons on the radio, and sneaked off to Bible studies with friends when I thought I could get away with it.

Some who have come to faith in Jesus from observant Jewish families as well as from other religions have been shunned or disowned by their relatives and communities. Though I was not booted from my home after I gave my life to the Lord, there was palpable division throughout my teenage years in my home regarding my new faith.

My faith survived, and even flourished, in the inhospitable climate. However, those years of solo Bible reading convinced me that God's best was community. Though I've been sorely tempted at times to join the exodus away from church, I couldn't mute the language used through the Bible about the communal, interdependent nature of our shared new life in Christ. We are the body. We are living stones. We are the bride. When the church is truly the church, there is nothing more beautiful on the face of this earth. Yes, I've witnessed lots of dysfunction over the years, but I have also glimpsed what the church can and should be.

I've learned God's grace is present for the sick, the imprisoned, and the persecuted who can't be a part of a local congregation. God's grace is there for believers wounded by church dysfunction who need space and time away from church so they can begin to heal. He was there with me when I was a congregation of one, worshiping him alone in my room as a teen.

My Bible reading during those lonely years painted a powerful picture for me of church-as-family throughout the New

Testament. I leaned hard on the hope that when I was no longer living at home, the church would become the family I'd left behind.

Once I was free as an adult to attend church, my longing to belong and my extroverted personality left me vulnerable to the temptation to people-please, and cultivated a bit of socially acceptable idolatry within me. I did whatever I could to fit in to my new, strange family. Over the years, I volunteered for everything from running vacation Bible school to folding bulletins to staining baseboards for a new building.

Most of my efforts looked very spiritual. As I performed for others so I could gain their love and acceptance, I may have appeared spiritual, but the false gods of church and family drove some of my activities. My love for God was mixed with my unvoiced fear that I'd never find a place in a family, like wheat and tares growing together in the same soul.

Church splits and dysfunction have winnowed those tares through the years. At midlife, I found myself in a counselor's office seeking help dealing with depression and grief stemming from the recent deaths of my parents, the emptying of the nest, and the shock of yet another relocation. During our sessions, the counselor helped me process those losses, but also focused on things I'd never truly grieved, such as the relational and emotional losses I'd experienced in my family of origin after I'd come to faith in Jesus, as well as the smaller, but still significant, losses I'd experienced through church upheaval. I discovered that those unprocessed losses helped to fuel my need-to-be-needed motivations and shaped my sometimes unrealistic expectations of my fellow church members. God wasn't asking me to "forget" (as if that were possible!) or deny that those experiences happened, but instead to allow Him to transform those experiences into the kind of wisdom and experience I'd need for the next leg of my pilgrimage.

He doesn't invite people to follow Him because they're baggage-free. He calls us to follow because He loves us too much to leave us as we were.

ON THE ROAD WITH JESUS

The word for "follow" used most often in the gospels is *akoloutheo* (ak-ol-oo-theh'-o), which comes from the words for "union" and "road."[2] Akoloutheo is a word describing someone who joins themselves heart, soul, mind, and strength as a disciple to a leader or guide. It describes purposeful movement and intimate relationship. Akoloutheo captures the essence of what a believer's pilgrimage is.

Akoloutheo was a fairly common word in the first century. When Jesus spoke it, He used it to paint a picture of two-way commitment: His complete, perfect loyalty to His disciples, and the all-in devotion Jesus expected from those following Him. The word also connotes motion. Following joins you to the road Jesus is walking.

There has been a long pattern in evangelical churches of speaking of salvation as a single moment in time. And it is. But it's also so much more. We've been imprinted with lasting images of a pastor asking the congregation to bow heads and close eyes as he prays a simple prayer inviting not-yet-believers to invite Jesus into their lives or people streaming forward to the altar to receive Christ at the end of a Billy Graham crusade.

My own story is marked by this kind of single darkness-to-light moment. When I was a young believer, I was sure my prayer asking God to save and forgive me was the single most important moment in my life, sealing my fate for all eternity. While it was a crucial moment, I eventually realized that every moment carries the weight of decision: Will I follow Him here and now?

There are many of us who don't have a dramatic "once lost, now found" moment like mine as part of their faith story. Whether we have a turning point experience or quietly grow in the faith throughout our lives, each one of us must respond to the call to follow Jesus heart, soul, mind, and strength in this moment.

Pilgrimage is always a step-by-step decision to follow Him. Those steps may look like repentance as we turn toward Him from a place we've wandered after choosing to rebel against God. They may look like obedience, as we continue to track His steps as we face the challenge of the narrow road. They may look like fellowship, as we commune with Him on the journey.

But they will always look like death:

> Then Jesus said to his disciples, "Whoever wants to be my disciple must deny themselves and take up their cross and follow me. For whoever wants to save their life will lose it, but whoever loses their life for me will find it. What good will it be for someone to gain the whole world, yet forfeit their soul? Or what can anyone give in exchange for their soul?" (Matt. 16:24–26)

This is the kind of akoloutheo to which we're called as followers of Jesus. His first-century audience didn't need much exposition about what this meant. The cross, a symbol of torture and death, was an instantly-recognizable image to them. The cross was reserved as an instrument of execution for those deemed by authorities to be criminals. The guilty one would be stripped of everything that marked his identity: his reputation, his worldly possessions, his family and friends, and even his clothes. Shamed and scorned, he would then carry the wooden crossbar, and in many cases, the entire cross, through the streets before being hammered onto it and left to die a public, grueling death.

A. W. Tozer translates for us moderns what the cross means in our lives: "The cross is the suffering the Christian endures as a consequence of his following Christ in perfect obedience. Christ chose the cross by choosing the path that led to it; and it is so with His followers. In the way of obedience stands the cross, and we take the cross when we enter that way."[3]

At the time Jesus said these words to His disciples, He was in the thick of His ministry in Galilee. No one hearing Him speak would have ever imagined this wonderful teacher and miracle worker would be headed for the very cross of which He spoke.

Author David Platt captured the essence of Jesus' intentions for His followers:

> Let's put ourselves in the shoes of the eager followers of Jesus in the first century....
>
> This is where we come face to face with a dangerous reality. We *do* have to give up everything we have to follow Jesus. We *do* have to love him in a way that makes our closest

relationships in this world look like hate....

But we don't want to believe it. We are afraid of what it might mean for our lives....

And this is where we need to pause. Because we are starting to redefine Christianity. We are giving in to the dangerous temptation to take the Jesus of the Bible and twist him into a version of Jesus we are more comfortable with....

But do you and I realize what we are doing at this point? We are molding Jesus into our image. He is beginning to look a lot like us because, after all, that is whom we are most comfortable with. And the danger now is that when we gather in our church buildings to sing and lift up our hands in worship, we may not actually be worshiping the Jesus of the Bible. Instead we may be worshiping ourselves.[4]

Jesus knows our human propensity for looking backward toward the past to try to tabulate the cost of following Him. Here's the thing: if our past was uncompromised and overflowing with vibrant spiritual health, He wouldn't need to tell us to follow Him. We would have already been "pilgrimming" instead of wandering.

Scripture's first vivid example of this truth is found in Genesis 19:1–29, the story of the destruction of the sister towns of Sodom and Gomorrah. Abraham's nephew Lot was living in these towns that had become cesspools of sin. Abraham had interceded with God on behalf of Sodom, asking God to spare the city where his nephew Lot was living if God could find even ten righteous men living there (Gen. 18:16–33). Three male angelic visitors came to Sodom, and Lot invited them into his home.

Every man in the city appeared as a mob at Lot's door, demanding to have sex with his visitors. In a sign of desperation, Lot even volunteered to give his virgin daughters over to the crazed mob, but the ravening men insisted they wanted the visitors instead.

There weren't ten righteous men in Sodom and Gomorrah. They'd turned from their Creator *en masse* and created a culture of flagrant disregard for His ways. God told Lot to gather his family and flee because He was going to give Sodom and Gomorrah what they'd been telling Him with their rebellion they truly desired—death. God was going to rain sulfurous fire on the entire region.

Lot obeyed. While his family was on the road heading toward refuge, Scripture tells us Lot's wife looked back and experienced the same destruction as was being visited on her former home (Gen. 19:26). This look back was not a quick glance. Despite the fact the stench from sulfur and the smoke filling the air as it rose from dying bodies told her everything she needed to know about what was happening behind her, she looked back. The word used in the text, *nabat*, suggests this was an extended, studied gaze. What was she aching to see?

You cannot accurately count the cost of following Jesus if you are beholding your past in this sort of gaze. Luke 9:57–62 records Jesus' encounter with three would-be followers who were trying to do this very thing. The first man presented himself as a potential spiritual tourist to Jesus. Jesus confronted this by telling him he'd have to quit the idea of having a comfortable home and bed waiting for him when he was done with his adventure. The second man expressed willingness to follow Jesus after he first returned home to bury his father. The text doesn't tell us whether the man's father was on his deathbed or hale and hearty with many years of life still ahead of him. Jesus' response to him unmasked his subtle idolatry of his family and challenged him to pursue his true calling. The third man tells Jesus he just wants to say goodbye to his relatives, quick as a bunny, thus clearing his calendar of all further obligations. His offer to follow Jesus sounds like it is hampered by little more than a momentary delay. Jesus challenges him regarding his desire to script the timeline for his obedience.

Following requires us to watch who we're tracking and where we're going, not where we've been. Our past matters, but it will not automatically transform us into pilgrims.

There are those who will default to their church affiliation as the signifier of their commitment to God. That affiliation can tell a story about where you choose to spend some of your time each week, and perhaps where you serve and give. But it does not confer pilgrim status on you.

The tricky part of this equation is that we must respond to Him as individuals, but as we do, we become a part of the community of called-out ones known as the church. We must hold both in tension. Whether your local congregation is vibrant or on life-support, that institution cannot decide for you whether you will be a spiritual wanderer, tourist, settler, or pilgrim. That choice remains yours alone. But the moment you take that step, your identity becomes inextricably linked with the community of all the other pilgrims journeying on Jesus' narrow road (Matt. 7:13–14).

This identity is formed and tested in the context of community. The call to follow may be to stay in a congregation going through turmoil. For others in the same congregation, faithful following may mean searching for a new church home. In a time of upheaval in most every stream within the church and dizzying shifts in our culture, we may be tempted either to look to the past for guidance, or search for the exit ramp so we can go it alone. Both speak to our desire for comfort and security.

Neither leads us to the cross.

To consider

1. David Platt said, "... when we gather in our church buildings to sing and lift up our hands in worship, we may not actually be worshiping the Jesus of the Bible. Instead we may be worshiping ourselves." How might this be true? What would it look like if we truly worshiped the Jesus of the Bible?

2. How can nostalgia for "the good ol' days" obscure what God is doing here and now?

3. The cross was a state-sanctioned instrument of death in the first century. What are some ways in which people are put to death by governments today? Consider how you might reimagine Jesus' words about the cross by putting them in a modern context. What does it mean to deny yourself and lose your life as you follow Jesus?

To pray

Gracious Father, I confess I would like to set my own agenda for following You. I want to be a tourist, enjoying Instagram-ready adventure. I want to be able to obey when it is convenient. I want to follow when it is comfortable. I want to nurture my romantic notions of what the past could have been, rather than living for You in the here and now.

So long as I cling to my big ideas about what I think my life is supposed to look like, I will wander. So long as I allow other people or institutions to tell me who I am and where I'm going, I will wander. Help me find my place among Your pilgrim people.

Jesus, Your sacrifice on the cross reveals to me my deeply rooted desire for self-preservation. Your resurrection empowers me to pick up my own cross and start walking. I long to follow You in the same way a sheep follows its shepherd. To that end, I pray this pilgrim song:

> The LORD is my shepherd, I lack nothing.
>> He makes me lie down in green pastures,
> he leads me beside quiet waters,
>> he refreshes my soul.
> He guides me along the right paths
>> for his name's sake.
> Even though I walk
>> through the darkest valley,
> I will fear no evil,
>> for you are with me;

your rod and your staff, they comfort me.
You prepare a table before me
  in the presence of my enemies.
You anoint my head with oil;
  my cup overflows.
Surely your goodness and love will follow me
  all the days of my life,
and I will dwell in the house of the Lord
  forever. (Ps. 23)

I pray these words in the name of the Father, Son, and Spirit.

Amen.

CHAPTER 10

DIVERTED

We homeschooled our three children during the 1990s. The number one question I was asked by family members and strangers alike was, "What about socialization?" Most well-meaning inquirers couldn't understand how a child could learn to get along in the world without the immersive experience of a classroom environment.

Back then, people in the homeschool movement tended to possess (and express!) extremely strong convictions. Those convictions empowered parents to make what was then a relatively nonconformist educational choice for their family. I remember with great fondness some of the intelligent, creative families I knew who did a great job balancing academics, socialization, and discipleship. These homeschoolers sought to give their children the best education they could while at the same time being intentional about helping their children have meaningful engagement with the great big world around them.

There was another group of people in the homeschool world during the '90s. Though they were a relatively small percentage of the community, they tended to dominate the conversation whenever homeschool families gathered. These fiery, seemingly super-spiritual people harbored deep distrust of culture, government and, in many cases, most churches as well. They relished being strangers in a strange world. As a result, they created an alternative subculture that shut out as much worldly influence as possible. For many of them, this meant the home schooling lifestyle was defined by super-large families, home birth, long skirts, home businesses, and courtship instead of dating for the teen children.[1]

This latter group of homeschoolers with the big convictions and stubbornly alternative lifestyles were self-appointed exemplars of what it meant to be "in the world, not of the world" (John 17:14–17). They presented themselves as the *de facto* moral voice of the homeschool community, and it seemed to many of us who interacted with them that these families possessed an iron-clad guarantee their kids would never, ever go rogue. Or prodigal.

There have always been believers who've diverted from the culture so they could preserve their souls and nurture their faith. One well-known contemporary example of this includes the Amish and Old-Order Mennonites. Though these groups are often treated as a modern-day tourist attraction because of their horse and buggy transport, electricity-free households, and 1700s-style garb, they make those choices to declare to themselves and others that they are exiles from this world via their countercultural lifestyle.

As Western culture has continued to move away from its anchor in Judeo-Christian tradition, there has been an increased call by some conservative commentators for committed Jesus-followers to own their exile status within that culture. Orthodox Christian writer Rod Dreher exemplified this thinking in his book *The Benedict Option: A Strategy for Christians in a Post-Christian Nation*. He urged separation from culture and intentional Christian community as a saltlike preservative designed to save the faith of both adherents and Western civilization itself. He recalls philosopher Alasdair MacIntyre, who believed

> the time was coming when men and women of virtue would understand that continued full participation in mainstream society was not possible for those who wanted to live a life of traditional virtue. These people would find new ways to live in community, he said, just as Saint Benedict, the sixth-century father of Western monasticism, responded to the collapse of Roman civilization by founding a monastic order.[2]

Dreher suggests an exile's survival may depend on, among other things, choosing intentional community among people who share your faith and values; ordered, frequent corporate worship and daily family prayer; downshifting away from political activism; and either homeschooling or enrolling children in private schools committed to a classical model of Christian education. While I generally agreed with a good measure of Dreher's cultural analysis and could affirm his call to community and family-based discipleship, I found myself unsettled by the fact that I'd heard most of these ideas offered up as a foolproof formula by many of the leading voices in the homeschool community a generation ago.

Formulas may work in math class, but real life in a rebel world is rarely that simple.

Writer Luke Harrington observed, "That's the thing about following Jesus, though—it means you're rarely going to have a cultural army on your side. Jesus himself was born into a world rocked by culture war, and he never really embraced the cause of the conservatives (Sadducees), or the liberals (Pharisees), or the radicals (Zealots), or even the . . . Benedict-Option-types (Essenes). Instead he called them all to the same thing: 'Repent and follow me.'"[3]

IN THE WORLD, NOT OF THE WORLD

Many religious experts in the first century excelled at creating their own subculture within a culture they rightly believed was not their home. By the time Jesus was born, the Chosen People had been living again in part of the Promised Land for nearly five centuries, since the official end of the Babylonian exile. However, most of those years had been marked by occupation by other nations. There was no true peace, nor was there a descendant of David on the throne (1 Kings 2:4; 1 Chron. 22:10).

Righteousness for those religious experts was marked by scrupulously keeping both the Law and the countless other statutes they'd created to form fences around the Law. They added these extra measures so they could guarantee their obedience to God. Instead of being lights to the nations, they hoarded the light God gave them under the bushel basket of their own insular, superspiritual community (Isa. 49:6).

Most of Jesus' confrontational exchanges with the Pharisees were about calling them from the exile of the bushel basket and into pilgrimage. One of His final interactions with them included His pronouncement in Matthew 23:13–39 of seven woes over the way in which they'd lived. The word "woe" is both the expression of a broken heart and a prophetic declaration meant to be a call to repentance. Jesus was heartbroken that these leaders who truly desired to serve God had become experts in missing the point. His woes were a list of charges meant to turn them back to their first love:

- They were hypercontrolling, keeping everyone—even themselves—from being a part of God's kingdom.
- They expended tremendous energy to convert a single person to their clique and had turned that person into a clone of themselves instead of helping that person become a follower of God.
- They made foolish vows, trying to sanctify their broken promises by linking their words to sacred items in the temple.
- They were scrupulous in their attention to minutiae, but lax in the things closest to God's heart—justice, mercy, and faithfulness.
- They obsessed about appearing holy to everyone else, but neglected to care for their souls, which were teeming with greed and self-indulgence.

- They focused on externals, while rotting with hypocrisy from the inside out.
- They revered heroes from the past and claimed they were spiritual descendants of those people. Yet they neglected to realize their own testimony aligned them with the very people who put those righteous prophets to death.

Throughout His ministry, Jesus made no secret of the fact that His disciples were going to be seen by others as different (John 15:18–19; 17:16). Though He called His followers to a righteousness that exceeded that of the religious elites, Jesus wasn't demanding they exist shrink-wrapped in protective holiness as exiles from this world. Instead, He invited them to express their restored relationship with God by pouring themselves into the lives of others.

In Luke 10:1–23, Jesus chooses seventy-two[4] from His growing group of followers to travel ahead of Him in pairs to prepare the people for His visit. He gives them a series of simple, sobering instructions before sending them out: be wise, remain morally pure, travel light, stay focused on your mission, be discerning, be gracious, serve generously, proclaim the kingdom of God.

When this group came back from this "practice pilgrimage" rejoicing that they'd witnessed demons submitting to them, Jesus told them to focus their rejoicing instead on the reality that their names were written in heaven.

And then He joined their rejoicing. "At that time Jesus, full of joy through the Holy Spirit, said, 'I praise you, Father, Lord of heaven and earth, because you have hidden these things from the wise and learned, and revealed them to little children. Yes,

Father, for this is what you were pleased to do" (Luke 10:21). The word used in the text for "little children" is *nepios,* which refers to a baby or young child, but is also used to signify those who are unskilled, untrained people (1 Cor. 1:26–29). In other words, it was not their spiritual expertise that brought pleasure to Jesus, but their glad obedience.

Jesus' entire life was a pilgrimage. He came to seek and save the lost (Luke 19:10). After His resurrection, He launched each one of His followers out into the world in His footsteps as pilgrims:

> Then Jesus came to them and said, "All authority in heaven and on earth has been given to me. Therefore go and make disciples of all nations, baptizing them in the name of the Father and of the Son and of the Holy Spirit, and teaching them to obey everything I have commanded you. And surely I am with you always, to the very end of the age." (Matt. 28:18–20)

There is much wrapped into these words—repentance, holiness, invitation into community with the Triune One, the call to make disciples, and the emphasis that we do not journey alone. He is with us every step of the way. While this passage is often quoted by church leaders to spark evangelism or send missionaries, Jesus does not put any limits on who is supposed to hear and do what He says. These are pilgrim words.

Saul the Pharisee had spent his life focusing on not being contaminated by the sinful world around him. Acts 9:1–18 records Saul's encounter with the risen Jesus on the road to Damascus. Some time after this, Saul, whose name meant "inquired of God," began to be referred to as Paul, which means "humble" and certainly matched his new station in life (see Acts 13:9).

Reviled by most of his former friends, Paul eventually became a leader in the young church. He spent a good part of his life among the Gentiles—the people he'd spent most of his early life avoiding. He coached believers to see themselves as exiles in relation to their own sinful behavior: "Dear friends, I urge you, as foreigners and exiles, to abstain from sinful desires, which wage war against your soul. Live such good lives among the pagans that, though they accuse you of doing wrong, they may see your good deeds and glorify God on the day he visits us" (1 Peter 2:11–12). He was not counseling them to exile themselves from the world around them.

This engagement with the world is meant to be as multifaceted and diverse as the body of Christ is. Some of us are activists. Others are more contemplative. But all of us are called to participate in the great adventure of following Jesus and making disciples.

Carlo Carretto was a twentieth-century monk who lived a life of extreme monasticism in the North African desert for more than a decade, seeking God in solitude and living a life devoted to prayer. After visiting his mother in Italy, Carretto was struck with the realization that she was far more contemplative than he was though she'd been busy running a household and raising a family. Writer Ron Rolheiser said of Carretto: "What this taught was not that there was anything wrong with what he had been doing in living as a hermit. The lesson was rather that there was something wonderfully right about what his mother had been doing all these years as she lived the interrupted life amidst the noise and incessant demands of small children. He had been in a monastery, but so had she."[5]

INTO THIS WORLD?

Our world at times is coarse, confusing, terrifying, and dangerous. (It is also beautiful.) Most of us feel powerless when we read the headlines or watch the news. Too often, our lives and communities are affected by decisions made somewhere else by people we've never met. There are wars and rumors of wars, natural disasters, and the simmering uncertainty of when a radicalized, bomb-wearing individual might decide to detonate themselves in the middle of a sporting event.

I recognize the yearning to escape from it all. The desire to protect our children amplifies those concerns. I've felt the longing to shield my kids and to hide my family from the big, bad world. Our responsibility as parents is to do all we can to protect our kids from harm as we seek to disciple them in the way of Jesus. Love for them and for the One who gave them to us compels us to do both.

Not long ago, I ran into Annie, one of my old homeschool compatriots. We traded notes about what our adult children were doing. She observed that few of the kids we knew back in the day were coloring in the lines their parents had drawn for them when they were young. A fair percentage of them had chosen to pursue a different lifestyle or partner than their parents planned for them. Some were no longer walking with Christ. With great sadness, Annie told me she'd assumed homeschooling would give her a button she could push in her children's lives to ensure they'd always stay on the straight and narrow. As they'd become adults and begun making their own decisions, she was shocked to discover there was no button.

Jesus chastised the Pharisees for building their lives around the idea of a button—a formula that would guarantee a happy outcome. There is nothing new under the sun. Whether it's a strict lifestyle designed to keep the world at bay or innocuous-sounding messages or books that promise "Seven Steps to a Happy Marriage" or "How You Can Have a Winning Family," the notion of a formula is a lure for most of us. Our formulas reflect a sense that a God-honoring life will require extra effort. But these "outside in" remedies fall short of God's purpose for us. He desires us to be holy, and that can only happen from the inside out—in each one of us as individuals and among all of us who are walking the narrow road with Jesus.

The prophet Ezekiel prophesied to Judah that God himself would give them a born-again ability to obey Him: "I will give you a new heart and put a new spirit in you; I will remove from you your heart of stone and give you a heart of flesh" (Ezek. 36:26). We see this very thing happening at Pentecost, as the Holy Spirit is poured out on this new community, the church (Acts 2). Their hearts aflame, the early church spread the good news like wildfire in a hostile, pagan world. Their single-minded love for God led to the kinds of lives that set them apart from their culture, while simultaneously leading them into it. They didn't participate in sin. They were seeking to live as citizens of the kingdom of God, so it automatically set them at odds with those around them, leading to fierce persecution as well as re-markable growth in the church.

It wasn't until after Christianity became the official state-sanctioned religion of the Roman Empire in AD 380 that a stream of fiery believers first chose to separate from the majority culture, heading out to live a monastic life in the desert. They chose exile from what they viewed as a spiritually compromised society so they could continue their pilgrim journey. While some engaged in what we might see as extreme forms of spiritual self-discipline out in the wilderness, most were simply committed to a single-minded pursuit of the God they loved. The words of Theodoros of Thebes capture the humility and passion for God of those who joined the out-to-the-desert movement: "Neither in our heart nor in our mouth had we anything other than the word of God alone, and we did not feel we were living on earth but were celebrating in heaven."[6] It is worth noting that this movement didn't really gain steam until the church became the state religion.

Writer Bradley Nassif explained,

Under Emperor Constantine, large numbers joined the church for the social privileges it bestowed. Many sought status and prosperity more than the cross. The influx of nominal Christians made the church a spiritually sick institution, and a radical illness called for a radical remedy. Ordinary men and women, most of them illiterate, heard the death-call of the gospel and responded by fleeing to the desert to live out their calling, either alone or in community. Peasants, shepherds, camel traders, former slaves, and prostitutes were the first to go.[7]

A desire for self-preservation is a reaction against a decaying culture. A reaction is not a calling—and it is not an option for a pilgrim. We walk toward God not in reaction, but in response to His invitation to follow, no matter where He leads.

To consider

1. Have you known people who've opted for extreme forms of separation from the world? What has been your experience with them?

2. How do you balance the tension between being in the world, but not of the world (John 17:14–15)? Can you give an example of a time when you've had to make a difficult choice in this regard? What counsel would you give to a new believer about how to obey this command of Jesus?

3. How would you describe the faith of a person who is reacting against toxic cultural trends versus the faith of someone who is responding to the call of God? Are there times when reaction can be a healthy response to a decaying culture? If so, when?

_____

_____

_____

_____

_____

_____

_____

_____

_____

_____

_____

To pray

Dear Jesus, I am unsure how to walk the narrow road between being in this world but not of it. There are times when I want to blend in with the majority culture around me. I don't want to be different. There are other times when I wish I could run far, far away from the everyday coarseness of a world determined to revel in its exile from You. It seems so much easier to look for a formula that will either allow me to blend in or escape.

Please guide me, Lord. Help me to root my life in You. Your Word tells me that a pilgrim's life is anchored in obedience to God and is both resilient and flourishing. You tell me it is possible to live this way:

> Blessed is the one
> who does not walk in step with the wicked
> or stand in the way that sinners take
> or sit in the company of mockers,
> but whose delight is in the law of the LORD,
> and who meditates on his law day and night.
> That person is like a tree planted by streams of water,
> which yields its fruit in season
> and whose leaf does not wither—
> whatever they do prospers. (Ps. 1:1–3)

I seek You as I walk the impossibly narrow road between "in the world" and "not of the world." I desire to glorify You every step I take, Jesus.

Amen.

CHAPTER 11

REVEALED

I think I'm about to lose my job," my husband said. During his long career in Information Technology, Bill had worked for both large multinational corporations and small businesses. He'd faced possible layoffs before but had always survived the cuts.

March 2017 was different. The day after he predicted he was about to be laid off, he walked in the door midday with his jacket slung over his arm, carrying a small box of his office bric-a-brac.

We were a couple of weeks into his search for a new position when I noticed a strange swelling in a lymph node under one arm. I knew I was at higher risk for breast cancer than the average woman as I'm an Ashkenazi Jew (there's a strong genetic link in my population), my mom died of breast cancer, and I was diagnosed a couple of years ago with a rare immune system deficiency, which affects my ability to fight off infections and cancers.

I went for a mammogram, which led to a sonogram because the radiologist saw something suspicious on the results. The diagnostic tests produced more murky outcomes, and doctors called for a biopsy to be scheduled. Being ever the optimist, I was well into the process of planning my funeral service as the procedure was taking place when I heard the physician say one of the most beautiful sentences in the English language: "It's benign."

The relief and gratitude carried me for a few days, but quickly eroded as we assessed our housing situation. We were living in a rental house that had been plagued with an infestation of black mold and had serious electrical and plumbing problems, having lost the home we once owned in the wake of the 2007–2008 housing market collapse. The cost of housing in our area was quite pricey. We faced yet another move in our long life together of moving to new places, this time to somewhere cheaper, but who would rent to us without a steady income source?

As if on cue, a beloved prodigal in our lives who'd been a source of great sorrow and much prayer over the years called us asking for money. Though we wouldn't have chosen to assist with this situation even if we had the funds, the heartbreaking phone calls further amplified our dizzying state of affairs.

Sometimes, our bodies narrate what is happening in our souls. Not long after that difficult phone call, I stepped outside on the rain-slicked, mossy deck of our rental home, slipped, and heard the sickening pop of my knee dislocating and the crunch of bones breaking in both knee and tailbone. Surgery to repair the knee was followed by serious complications. Healing has been slow and painful.

If I was secretly harboring any Instagram-worthy images of pilgrimage before this, these difficult months have exorcised them from my imagination. Instead, the three strands that have defined the notion of pilgrimage for generations of believers— moral, physical, and interior journeys toward union with the Lord—have for me become a single braided cord through which I understand who I truly am as I limp through this series of trials and tests. Can I trust Him even when I don't understand why these things are happening? Will I follow Him even though it hurts? And do I have eyes to see His perfect care and abundant provision for me through it all?

Each of the three pilgrimage themes runs through Scripture from beginning to end. For instance, I see moral pilgrimage high-lighted when God gave the Law to Moses in the Sinai Desert and when Ezra read the Law aloud to the community as they were rebuilding Jerusalem. I hear it in the words of Jesus as He showed and told His followers that their righteousness must exceed that of the Pharisees (Matt. 5:20).

Physical pilgrimage imprinted the Chosen People from the time of the Exodus and became a part of their yearly experience as they gathered in Jerusalem at the temple for Passover, Shavuot, and Sukkot each year. And Jesus' journey to the cross embodied physical pilgrimage for all of us.

The interior pilgrimage is highlighted in the flesh-and-blood portraits throughout Scripture of humans in relationship with God. My favorite example is the unvarnished story of the shep-herd boy anointed to be king of Israel, David. The Bible shows us both his deep desire for God and the ways in which David wandered from Him. We see in his story the innocence of a youngest son, singing to God in pure joy as he tended his father's flocks; a young man on the run, clinging to the One who was guiding his journey away from his enemy; and the adult cries of a man confessing his sin to his Maker and Redeemer (Pss. 32, 51, 86, 122).

This recent collection of challenges in my life has underscored just how flimsy the usual markers of identity can be. We Westerners are in the habit of understanding our identity by our roles and relationships in this world. Typically, we define ourselves by the way we answer questions like: What do you do for work? Where do you live? Are you married? Do you have children? Where did you go to school?

A pilgrim is formed by the question "Do I trust Him?" At some point in our journey with Jesus, most of us will face some form of suffering. It may be persecution, grief, loss of health, or broken relationships. It is an unwelcome companion that can halt our journey as bitterness or anger derails us. Or it can propel us onward as it disconnects us from clinging to the identity markers given to us by the world. Suffering strips us of the illusion that we are the makers of our life's map. Pastor Tim Keller said, "When pain and suffering come upon us, we finally see not only that we are not in control of our lives but that we never were."[1]

We may face affliction as the result of the consequences of our poor or sinful choices, and it is good to recognize that God will use that kind of suffering as well. A vivid (and salty!) example: Georgi Readman in the UK chose to live on a diet of little more than ramen for more than a decade. Doctors told the severely malnourished teen she has the health of an eighty-year-old.[2] Even if our lives have been comprised of reckless decisions to this moment, God may use the natural consequences (like having an old woman's body as the result of a ramen-only diet) to discipline us, but He doesn't waste anything—not even our foolishness.

Suffering uproots us. The apostle Paul wrote his friends in Rome about the way in which suffering propels us from our regularly scheduled lives: "We also glory in our sufferings, because we know that suffering produces perseverance; perseverance, character; and character, hope" (Rom. 5:3–4). Perseverance is a word denoting forward motion; it is the determination to persist toward a goal despite roadblocks and opposition it faces.

Paul notes that perseverance forms moral character. He recognizes that only someone who is determined to pursue a life beyond the present moment's difficulties can understand the true nature of hope. In another of Paul's letters to a church facing both trials and temptations, he wrote, "For now we see only a reflection as in a mirror; then we shall see face to face. Now I know in part; then I shall know fully, even as I am fully known" (1 Cor. 13:12). Our "now" is not the sum and total of our story in God.

It's been said, "God brings men into deep waters not to drown them, but to cleanse them."[3] God uses suffering to purify us. Pastor Tim Keller notes, "So suffering is at the heart of the Christian faith. It is not only the way Christ became like and redeemed us, but it is one of the main ways we become like him and experience his redemption. And that means that our suffering, despite its painfulness, is also filled with purpose and usefulness."[4]

Suffering can purge us of our lesser loves, our puny idols, and our self-reliance if we allow it to do its work in us.

Jesus' healing and deliverance ministry was focused on those who were suffering. Even as He set people free in the present, He was pointing them toward a future destination. The Beatitudes, found in Matthew 5:3–12, outline what the rich blessing of hope looks like for one who has been launched into pilgrimage by suffering:

- Those who have suffered because they are needy of spirit are possessors of the kingdom of heaven.
- Those who suffer because of grief will be comforted.
- Those who suffer marginalization and neglect will inherit the earth.
- Those who suffer the effects of sin and find they long deeply for righteousness will be fully satisfied.
- Those who have suffered injustice but have chosen to demonstrate mercy will receive mercy in the future.
- Those who have suffered broken relationships but purpose to pursue reconciliation will be recognized as children of God.
- Those who have suffered persecution because of their faith in the Son will be honored citizens of the kingdom of heaven.

These promises Jesus made to those who are suffering find their climax in the final book of the Bible, Revelation. Some readers stay away from the book because of its arresting, perplexing prophetic imagery. Others put their energy into trying to decode the book's mysteries so they'll have the inside track on how the end of days will unfold. And others recognize in the book descriptions of history that's already come to pass.

I've approached the book in each of these ways during different seasons of my life, trying to make sense of its imagination-exploding angels and scrolls and warfare and worship. These days, it is most helpful for me to recognize in Revelation all the ways in which God's just love disciplines and purifies His community of followers as we journey homeward. If the Beatitudes describe what launches us as individuals into pilgrimage, Revelation illumines how the journey unfolds for the church as members of His beloved bride.

Revelation tells us that all wandering will cease. Suffering will end. The journey that began with "Follow me" will have its culmination here:

> Then I saw "a new heaven and a new earth," for the first heaven and the first earth had passed away, and there was no longer any sea. I saw the Holy City, the new Jerusalem, coming down out of heaven from God, prepared as a bride beautifully dressed for her husband. And I heard a loud voice from the throne saying, "Look! God's dwelling place is now among the people, and he will dwell with them. They will be his people, and God himself will be with them and be their God. 'He will wipe every tear from their eyes. There will be no more death' or mourning or crying or pain, for the old order of things has passed away." (Rev. 21:1–5)

This difficult year in my life has included plenty of tears and prayers like "Help, Lord," "Please make it stop," "Send Bill a job," and "Give us wisdom." God has revealed Himself to us through the care of others in His body. He has taught me in ever-deeper ways what it means to seek Him for our daily needs, continually relinquishing my anxiety about our future to Him (Matt: 6:11; 1 Peter 5:7). The definition of "hope" in circumstances like the ones my husband and I have faced this year can easily shrivel to the size of things that will bring short-term respite: I hope Bill can find a new full-time job; I hope my body will rebound from these injuries; I hope we can find an affordable place to live.

These are good desires, and we're grateful many friends have joined us in prayer for these things. But they are flimsy, impermanent things in which to fix my hope. When the author of Hebrews wrote to his suffering brothers and sisters, "Now faith is confidence in what we hope for and assurance about what we do not see" (Heb. 11:1), he was telling them that, as they oriented their hearts toward the One who was, and is, and is to come, their hope would become action, guiding them home. Pilgrimage comes to an end in union with the living God. Our pilgrim identity will fall from us like a husk as we emerge and revel in who we were created to be: His beloved.

Revelation concludes with that essence of pilgrimage with a warning and an invitation:

> The Spirit and the bride say, "Come!" And let the one who hears say, "Come!" Let the one who is thirsty come; and let the one who wishes take the free gift of the water of life.
>
> I warn everyone who hears the words of the prophecy of this scroll: If anyone adds anything to them, God will add to that person the plagues described in this scroll. And if anyone

takes words away from this scroll of prophecy, God will take away from that person any share in the tree of life and in the Holy City, which are described in this scroll.

He who testifies to these things says, "Yes, I am coming soon."

Amen. Come, Lord Jesus. (Rev. 22:17–20)

The word "come" in this text is *erchomai* (er'-khom-ahee). It is a fairly common word in the New Testament. It is used to denote that the "inviter," the "invitee," or both are arriving at a set destination. Even as Jesus has called us to follow Him, He tells us in pilgrim language that He is coming for us.[5]

His invitation to us to come to Him is met with the cry of a pilgrim's soul: "Come, Lord Jesus!" This is like call-and-response in music or certain kinds of sermons. A leader sings or speaks a phrase, and to answer, another person, choir, or congregation echoes the phrase or meaning. The very words that launch us from exile into pilgrimage are our journey's end. Jesus invites us. He Himself is the road we travel and is our companion on the way. And He is our destination, calling us to come to Him.

We were born to wander, but we are born again to wander home.

To consider

1. Pastor Tim Keller wrote, "When pain and suffering come upon us, we finally see not only that we are not in control of our lives but that we never were." What in life leads us to believe we are the masters of our destiny? How can pain and suffering change that narrative?

2. Some of us have difficulty in thinking about suffering because we compare our own experience to the suffering of others: "What's happening to me isn't as serious as what _____ is going through." Comparison is an unhelpful way in which to assess your experience. If you haven't faced suffering of some kind in your life, give God thanks. But if you have, consider what the experience has revealed to you about your character, God's character, and the way in which your suffering has informed your understanding about what hope is.

3. As you read the description of the end of the pilgrim journey in Revelation 21:5, how does it compare with the circumstances of your present life? What words or phrases from the passage are most meaningful to you personally right now? Why? What does this passage tell you about all of us who comprise the pilgrim church?

_____

_____

_____

_____

_____

_____

To pray

Jesus, give me ears to hear Your call—Follow Me. Please teach me to follow when the ground underneath my feet is smooth and level and the scenery pleasant. Teach me to follow when the road is unpaved and poorly marked.

And my Lord, teach me to follow when suffering comes. Help me to recognize while I'm in the midst of a dark, difficult time that you are using these experiences to purify me and sharpen my hope. This mystery is our strength in our times of suffering: You saw and enfolded Your followers in the joy You saw set before You even as You suffered on the cross for them. Thank you that I don't journey alone. Your Spirit companions me, instructs me, and comforts me as I walk with You. How I want this song from your Word to become my song:

> How lovely is your dwelling place,
>   LORD Almighty!
> My soul yearns, even faints,
>   for the courts of the Lord;
> my heart and my flesh cry out
>   for the living God.
> Even the sparrow has found a home,
>   and the swallow a nest for herself,
>   where she may have her young—
> a place near your altar,
>   LORD Almighty, my King and my God.
> Blessed are those who dwell in your house;
>   they are ever praising you.

Blessed are those whose strength is in you,
  whose hearts are set on pilgrimage. (Ps. 84:1–5)

This pilgrim path is how I become my truest self; where I become the one You created me to be. And so, my heart is set on pilgrimage. In the name of the Father, Son, and Holy Spirit, I pray: Please guide me home.

Come, Lord Jesus.

Amen.

ACKNOWLEDGMENTS

Though writing can be a solitary task, I have not journeyed through the writing of this book alone.

I am grateful for the essential prayers and support of those who've walked alongside me during the last year: the women of Digging Deeper, the Bible study group of which I am a part; my New Conversations friends; those in my two writer's communities, INK and Hermi; and those in an online theology group of which I'm a part. The encouragement from friends in each of these groups sustained me more than any of them can ever know.

The feedback from those who read various parts of my clumsy first drafts helped me write better final versions of the chapters in this book. A giant thank you to Carol Marshall and Margie Conner. And to my prayer partner of two decades, Meg Kausalik, who both interceded for me and cried with me during what was an incredibly difficult year in her life, I continue to be humbled and inspired by her steadfast faith. What a gift she's been in my life.

My agent, Dan Balow, not only helped this project find its home, but was supportive throughout the writing process. I have been awed by editor Ingrid Beck's belief in this project and in my voice as a writer.

At the end of 2016, Amanda Cleary Eastep approached me after I spoke at an event on the theme of pilgrimage. That brief conversation led to conversations on another topic close to my heart, spiritual growth at midlife and beyond, and led the two of us to launch a website featuring the voices of older women and men, ThePerennialGen.com. I was thrilled when Amanda told me she'd landed an editorial position at Moody Publishers—and stunned when she told me she'd been assigned this book to edit! I have a good imagination, but never could have dreamed one small conversation would connect our lives in so many ways. God's imagination is infinitely bigger than mine.

I am grateful for all I have learned from my children, Rachel, Ben, and Jacob, and my beloved grandsons, Gabriel and Lio. Each one is a gift to me.

I've lived the story of this book alongside my husband, Bill, who has walked with me for more than 38 years as of this writing. His faithfulness to God, our family, and me has urged me onward. *Ani ohevet otcha*—I love you.

To Jesus my Messiah, I don't have enough vocabulary to say thank You for all You've done for me. You are the way, the truth, and the life. I am following You all the way home.

FOR FURTHER READING

Here are a few books you may wish to consider if you're look-ing for some additional reading to encourage you on your pilgrim journey:

Bonhoeffer, Dietrich, *The Cost of Discipleship*. New York: Touch-stone, 1995. This book's unflinching truths about the reality of what it means to follow Jesus have challenged readers for generations.

Bunyan, John. Edited by Rosalie de Rosset. *Pilgrim's Progress: Moody Classic Edition*. Chicago: Moody, 2007. A lovely, read-able version of this essential text for your library.

Hunkin, Oliver. *Dangerous Journey: The Story of Pilgrim's Prog-ress*. Grand Rapids: Eerdmans, 1985. This volume is aimed at readers ages ten and up. The gorgeous illustrations make the familiar story come alive.

Keller, Timothy. *Walking With God through Pain and Suffering*. New York: Penguin Books, 2015. Keller's pastoral wisdom shines through the pages of this book on a theme with no easy answers.

Manion, Jeff. *The Land Between: Finding God in Difficult Transitions.* Grand Rapids: Zondervan, 2010. This volume offers practical help and insight on the disorienting process of change.

Michel, Jen Pollock. *Keeping Place: Reflections on the Meaning of Home.* Downers Grove, IL: InterVarsity Press, 2017. This beautifully written meditation is full of rich insight on the pilgrim topic of home.

Peterson, Eugene. *A Long Obedience in the Same Direction: Discipleship in an Instant Society.* Downers Grove, IL: InterVarsity Press, 1980, 2000. Peterson's observations drawn from the Psalms of Ascent remind us that a follower's journey with Jesus calls on us to respond to His call with perseverance and deep trust.

NOTES

Introduction

1. "Americans Moving at Historically Low Rates, Census Bureau Reports," United Census Bureau, November 16, 2016, https://www.census.gov/newsroom/press-releases/2016/cb16-189.html.

2. D'Vera Cohn and Rich Morin, "Who Moves? Who Stays Put? Where's Home?", Pew Research Center, updated December 29, 2008, http://www.pewsocialtrends.org/2008/12/17/who-moves-who-stays-put-wheres-home/.

3. "Figures at a Glance," Statistical Yearbook, The UN Refugee Agency, http://www.unhcr.org/en-us/figures-at-a-glance.html.

4. Jen Pollock Michel, *Keeping Place: Reflections on the Meaning of Home* (Downers Grove, IL: InterVarsity Press, 2017), loc. 248–49, Kindle.

5. Article #15, Christian History Institute, https://christianhistory institute.org/incontext/article/augustine/.

6. Dee Dyas, "Pilgrims and Pilgrimage: Pilgrims in Christianity," https://www.york.ac.uk/projects/pilgrimage/content/.

Chapter 1: Uprooted

1. To be fair and balanced, let the record show Noah wasn't a perfect saint, but a flesh-and-blood human being. After the flood, Scripture reports that at some point, Noah got himself drunk and passed out naked in his tent. See Genesis 9:20–28.

2. A diaspora existence was promised by God if His people disobeyed Him (see Lev. 26:33, Deut. 4:27, and Deut. 28:64 for a few examples). The prophets warned about this impending judgment (see Jer. 9:16, 19:7; Ezek. 5:10, 22:15) as well as the certainty of

God's ultimate restoration (Jer. 23:3–8; Ezek. 37:21–25, 39:28; Zeph. 3:19–20).

3. Rabbi Ken Spiro, "History Crash Course #67: The Miracle of Jewish History," March 10, 2002, http://www.aish.com/h/iid/48964091.html.

4. Tori Rodriguez, "Descendants of Holocaust Survivors Have Altered Stress Hormones," *Scientific American*, March 1, 2015, https://www.scientificamerican.com/article/descendants-of-holocaust-survivors-have-altered-stress-hormones/.

"Intergenerational Trauma: Understanding Natives' Inherited Pain," Indian Country Free Reports, https://indiancountrymedia network.com/free-reports/intergenerational-trauma-understand ing-natives-inherited-pain/.

Note that this field of study is still emerging, and the data is still being debated in the scientific community: Seema Yasmin, "Experts debunk study that found Holocaust trauma is inherited," *Chicago Tribune*, June 9, 2017, http://www.chicagotribune.com/lifestyles/health/ct-holocaust-trauma-not-inherited-20170609-story.html.

5. Stephen King, *Different Seasons: Four Novellas* (New York: Pocket Books/Simon & Shuster, 2017), 627.

6. Glenn E. Meyers, "Augustine's Restless Heart," CBN, http://www1.cbn.com/churchandministry/augustines-restless-heart.

Chapter 2: Sent

1. "Genesis 12:1," Bible Hub, http://biblehub.com/lexicon/genesis/12-1.htm.

2. Lech Lecha: "Get Yourself Going," Reb Jeff, October 9, 2013, http://www.rebjeff.com/blog/lech-lecha-get-yourself-going.

3. Dr. Nosson Chayim Leff, "Parshas Lech Lecha," 2005, https://torah.org/torah-portion/sfas-emes-5766-lechlecha-2/.

4. "What is the rock in Matthew 16:18?", https://www.gotquestions.org/upon-this-rock.html.

5. Søren Kierkegaard, *Kierkegaard's Writings, Volume XV: Upbuilding Discourses in Various Spirits* (Princeton, NJ: Princeton University Press, 2009), 218.

Chapter 3: Waylaid

1. "Joseph's Brothers Go to Egypt (Genesis 42)," https://bible.org/seriespage/5-joseph-s-brothers-go-egypt-genesis-42.

2. "Slavery in India," Free the Slaves, http://www.freetheslaves.net/where-we-work/india/.

3. "Pale of Settlement," Wikipedia, last edited on December 3, 2017, https://en.wikipedia.org/wiki/Pale_of_Settlement.

4. Warsan Shire, "Home," a poem, in *Long Journeys. African Migrants on the Road*, Robert Alessandro Triulzi and Lawrence McKenzie (Leiden: Brill, 2013), xi.

Chapter 4: Displaced

1. John Gardner Quotes, *Good Reads*, https://www.goodreads.com/quotes/429997-self-pity-is-easily-the-most-destructive-of-the-non-pharmaceutical.

2. Tryon Edwards, *The New Dictionary of Thoughts: A Cyclopedia of Quotations* (Chicago, IL: Ravenio Books, 2015). Found under "Man" category.

3. Quote from Martin Marty, September 1 entry, *Answers in the Heart: Daily Meditations For Men And Women Recovering From Sex Addiction* (New York: Simon and Schuster, 2011), September 1.

4. For example, the Egyptians worshiped the frog gods Hapi and Heqt, and were faced with the plague of frogs sent by God in Ex. 8:1–15. Each plague was a response by God to the specific false gods worshiped by the Egyptians. See "The 10 Plagues—Jehovah Versus the Gods of Egypt," Barnes' Bible Charts, http://www.biblecharts.org/oldtestament/thetenplagues.pdf.

5. Henri J. M. Nouwen, *The Life of the Beloved: Spiritual Living in a Secular World* (New York: Crossroad Publishing, 2002), 33.

6. Marlena Graves, *A Beautiful Disaster: Finding Hope in the Midst of Brokenness* (Grand Rapids: Brazos Press, 2014), 7.

Chapter 5: Warned

1. John Bunyan, "Grace Abounding to the Chief of Sinners; or, a Brief Relation of the Exceeding Mercy of God in Christ, to His Poor Servant John Bunyan," Christian Classics Ethereal Library, Sections 4 and 8, https://www.ccel.org/ccel/bunyan/grace.iv.html.

2. Tracy McKenzie, "Why the Pilgrims Really Came to America (hint, it wasn't religious freedom)," November 16, 2014, http://www.christianity.com/church/church-history/why-the-pilgrims-really-came-to-america-hint-it-wasn-t-religious-freedom.html.

3. Paul F. M. Zahl, *Grace in Practice: A Theology of Everyday Life* (Grand Rapids: Eerdmans, 2007), 36.

4. Dietrich Bonhoeffer, *The Cost of Discipleship* (New York: Touchstone, 1995), 45.

5. Jeff Manion, *The Land Between: Finding God in Difficult Transitions* (Grand Rapids: Zondervan , 2010), 161.

Chapter 6: Divided

1. The three festivals are Passover and Shavuot in the spring, and Sukkot in the fall. Leviticus 23 lists the seven major holy days/weeks of the Jewish worship cycle. My book *Moments & Days: How Our Holy Celebrations Shape Our Faith* (Colorado Springs: NavPress, 2015) details these holidays as well as offering an overview of the Christian calendar.

2. Commentators believe the name Jeroboam probably means "The People Increase," but may also carry the implication "To Strive." See "Jeroboam meaning," Abarim Publications, http://www.abarim-publications.com/Meaning/Jeroboam.html#.WTvyYxPyvfY.

3. Tim Keller, *Counterfeit Gods: The Empty Promises of Money, Sex, and Power, and the Only Hope That Matters* (New York: Penguin, 2009), Introduction, II.

4. Dan Bouchelle, "Ideal or Idol: Avoiding the Family Cult in Church," Confessions of a Former Preacher (blog), April 2, 2013, http://danbouchelle.blogspot.com/2013/04/ideal-or-idol-avoiding-family-cult-in.html.

5. Other verses in this vein include Matthew 10:34–39 and Mark 10:29–31.

6. Rich Robinson, "Did Jesus Teach the Disciples to Hate Their Parents?" Jews for Jesus, January 1, 2000, https://jewsforjesus.org/answers/did-jesus-teach-his-disciples-to-hate-their-parents/.

Chapter 7: Remembered

1. Peter Toon, "Remember, Remembrance," Bible Study Tools, http://www.biblestudytools.com/dictionaries/bakers-evangelical-dictionary/remember-remembrance.html.

2. Jen Pollock Michel, *Keeping Place: Reflections on the Meaning of Home* (Downers Grove, IL: InterVarsity Press, 2017), loc. 337–38, Kindle.

3. The Edomites were descendants of Esau (Gen. 25:23) who lived just east of Israel's territory. During his reign, David conquered them (2 Sam. 8:13). During the time of the divided kingdom, Edom regained some of their former military strength. By the time Judah fell, Edom, long a thorn in Israel's flesh, had allied with the Babylonians and participated in the conquest of Jerusalem.

4. Jeremiah 25 details this seventy-year period of deep discipline and exile for the people of Judah. During the captivity, Daniel reads Jeremiah's words, does some calculating, and realizes the time of exile was drawing to a close. He commits to fast and pray (Dan. 9), and received from the angel Gabriel additional insight as to the nature and purpose of those seven decades of exile. Daniel 9:24 says there is a fixed time "decreed for your people and your holy city to finish transgression, to put an end to sin, to atone for wickedness, to bring in everlasting righteousness, to seal up vision and prophecy and to anoint the Most Holy Place."

Chapter 8: Trekked

1. British Pilgrimage Trust, http://britishpilgrimage.org/.

2. Eugene Peterson, *A Long Obedience in the Same Direction: Discipleship in an Instant Society* (Downers Grove, IL: InterVarsity Press, 1980, 2000), 16.

3. Dan Hitchens, "Pilgrimages are back—with less Christianity," *The Spectator*, July 16, 2016, https://www.spectator.co.uk/2016/07/pilgrimages-are-back-with-less-christianity/#.

4. Ibid.

5. Phileena Heuertz, *Pilgrimage of a Soul: Contemplative Spirituality for the Active Life* (Downers Grove, IL; InterVarsity Press, 2010), 20.

6. Mark D. Roberts, "Thin Places: A Biblical Investigation," Patheos, 2012, http://www.patheos.com/blogs/markdroberts/series/thin-places/.

7. Eugene Peterson, *A Long Obedience in the Same Direction: Discipleship in an Instant Society* (Downers Grove, IL: InterVarsity Press, 2nd ed, 2000), 22.

8. Ibid, 43.

9. Ezra 5:1–3. Note: Haggai and Zechariah mentioned here are the same prophets who authored the Old Testament prophetic books bearing their respective names.

Chapter 9: Sojourned

1. For more about those who are disaffected with church, see *Church Refugees: Sociologists reveal why people are DONE with church but not their faith* by Josh Packard and Ashleigh Hope (Group, 2015) and "Meet Those Who 'Love Jesus but Not the Church,'" Barna, March 30, 2017, https://www.barna.com/research/meet-love-jesus-not-church/.

2. "Akoloutheo," Bible Study Tools, http://www.biblestudytools.com/lexicons/greek/nas/akoloutheo.html.

3. A. W. Tozer, *The Radical Cross: Living the Passion of Christ* (Chicago: Moody, 2015), 54.

4. David Platt, *Radical: Taking Back Your Faith from the American Dream* (Colorado Springs: Multnomah, 2010), 12–13.

Chapter 10: Diverted

1. The Duggar family, known for their now-defunct TLC network show "Nineteen Kids and Counting" attempted to give American TV audiences a positive, encouraging spin on this stream of the homeschooling movement. The show was cancelled in 2015 after the oldest brother's past molestation incidents were brought to light.

2. Rod Dreher, *The Benedict Option: A Strategy for Christians in a Post-Christian Nation* (New York: Penguin Publishing Group, 2016), 2.

3. Luke T. Harrington, "The Fake Kidnapping Scandal That Almost Destroyed a Megachurch Pioneer," Christ Pop Culture, March 10, 2017, https://christandpopculture.com/fake-kidnapping-scandal-almost-destroyed-megachurch-pioneer/?utm_content=buffer3921f&utm_medium=social&utm_source=twitter.com&utm_campaign=buffer.

4. Some Bible translations say seventy; most have notes including both numbers, citing a probable copyists' discrepancy.

5. Ron Rolheiser, "The Domestic Monastery," January 7, 2001, http://ronrolheiser.com/the-domestic-monastery/#.WcWI8NOGPbg.

6. "Sayings of the Desert Fathers," St. Andrew's Greek Orthodox Church, May 3, 2012, http://saintandrewgoc.org/home/2012/5/3/sayings-of-the-desert-fathers.html.

7. Quoted in Marlena Graves, *A Beautiful Disaster: Finding Home In The Midst of Brokenness* (Grand Rapids: Brazos, 2014), 8. Source for quote: Bradley Nassif, "The Poverty of Love," *Christianity Today*, 4/30/08, http://www.christianitytoday.com/ct/2008/may/11.34.html.

Chapter 11: Revealed

1. Timothy Keller, *Walking With God through Pain and Suffering* (New York: Penguin Books, 2015), 5.

2. Tracy Miller, "My strange ramen addiction: Teen eats just ramen noodles for 13 years," Daily News, April 10, 2013, http://www.nydailynews.com/life-style/health/teen-eats-ramen-noodles-13-years-article-1.1312782.

3. Quote is typically attributed to John Hill Aughey, a pastor who lived in the mid-1800s. A Google search led me to an earlier source: *Every Man's Monitor; Or The Universal Counsellor in Prose and Verse*, 17.

4. Keller, *Walking With God through Pain and Suffering*, 163.

5. Matthew 24, 25:13, Luke 12:40, John 14:1–3, Acts 1:10–11, Colossians 3:4, 1 Thessalonians 4:16–17, Titus 2:13, 2 Peter 3:10, to name just a few.

FEELING WORN THIN?
COME FIND REST.

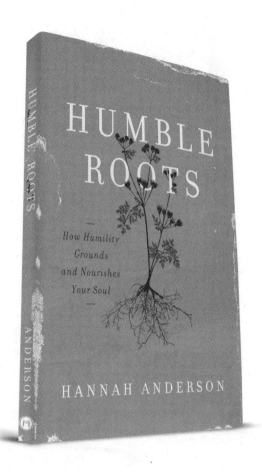

CAN GOD'S LOVE HURT?

A STORY OF TRAGEDY, TRUTH, AND REBELLIOUS HOPE

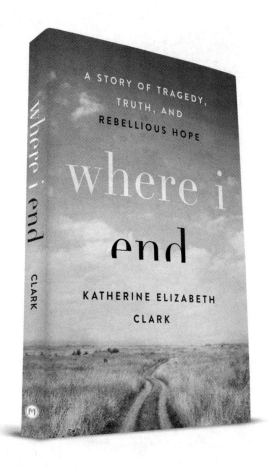

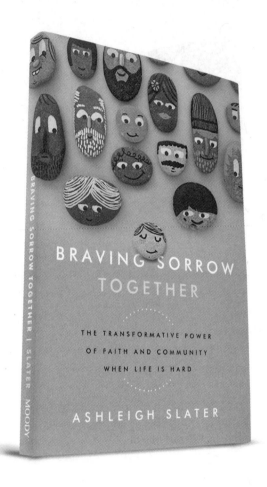